DISNEY

HANNAH MONTANA

TOKYOPOP®

Hamburg · London · Los Angeles · Tokyo

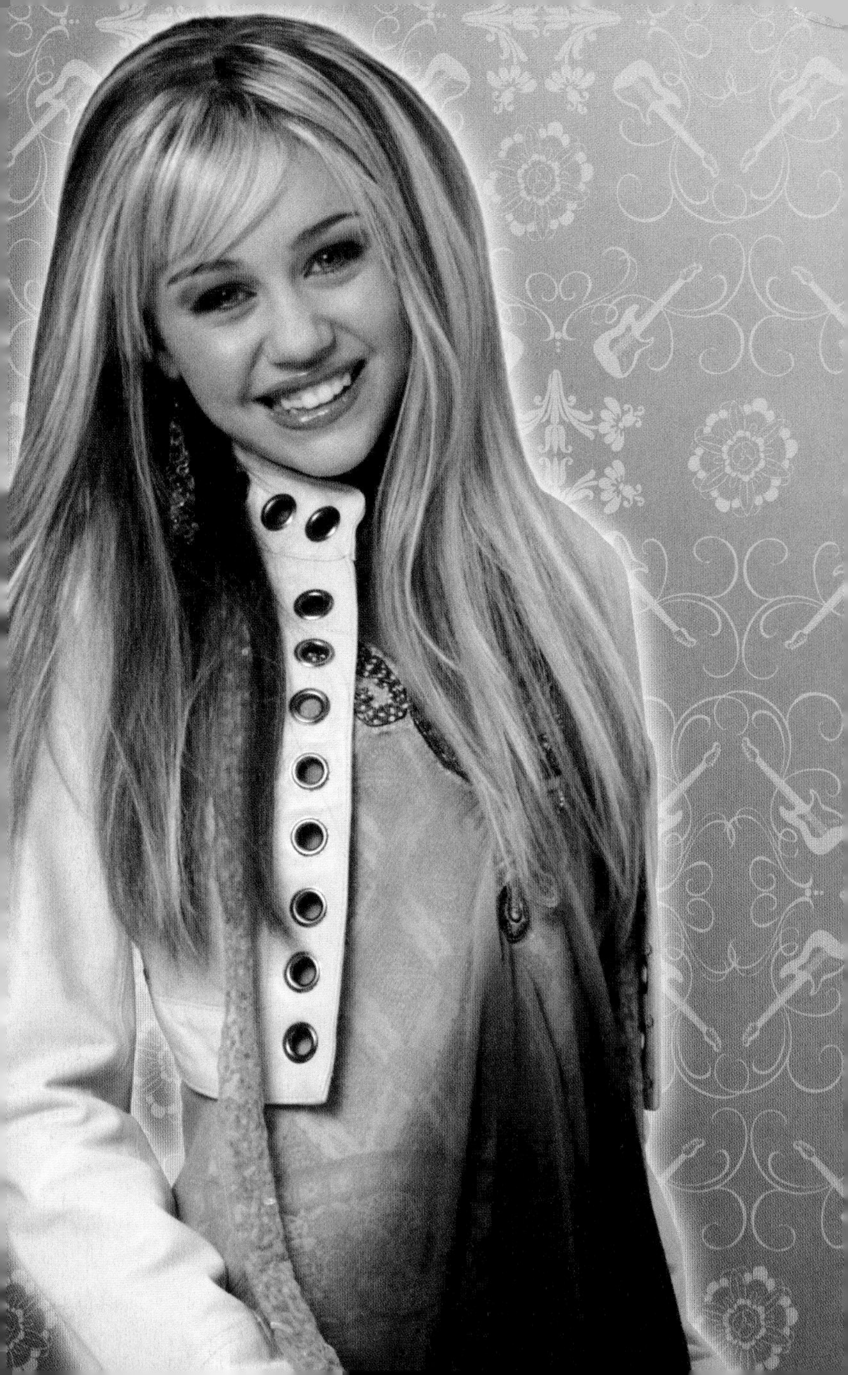

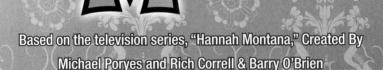

Disney
HANNAH MONTANA™

Based on the television series, "Hannah Montana," Created By
Michael Poryes and Rich Correll & Barry O'Brien

CRUSHES AND CAMPING

"Miley Get Your Gum"
Written By Michael Poryes

"Ooo, Ooo Itchy Woman"
Written By Steven Peterman & Gary Dontzig

Editor - Julie Taylor
Contributing Editors - Kimberlee Smith and Amy Court-Kaemon
Graphic Designer and Letterer - Monalisa J. de Asis
Cover Designer - Monalisa J. de Asis

Production Manager - Elisabeth Brizzi
Art Director - Anne Marie Horne
VP of Production - Ron Klamert
Editor in Chief - Rob Tokar
Publisher - Mike Kiley
President & C.O.O. - John Parker
C.E.O. & Chief Creative Officer - Stuart Levy

E-mail: info@TOKYOPOP.com
Come visit us online at www.TOKYOPOP.com

A  Cine-Manga® Book
TOKYOPOP Inc.
5900 Wilshire Blvd., Suite 2000
Los Angeles, CA 90036

Hannah Montana: Crushes and Camping
© 2007 Disney

ISBN: 978-1-4278-0282-8

First TOKYOPOP® printing: July 2007

10 9 8 7 6 5 4 3 2 1

Printed in the USA

DISNEY

HANNAH MONTANA™

CRUSHES AND CAMPING

CONTENTS

WHO'S WHO

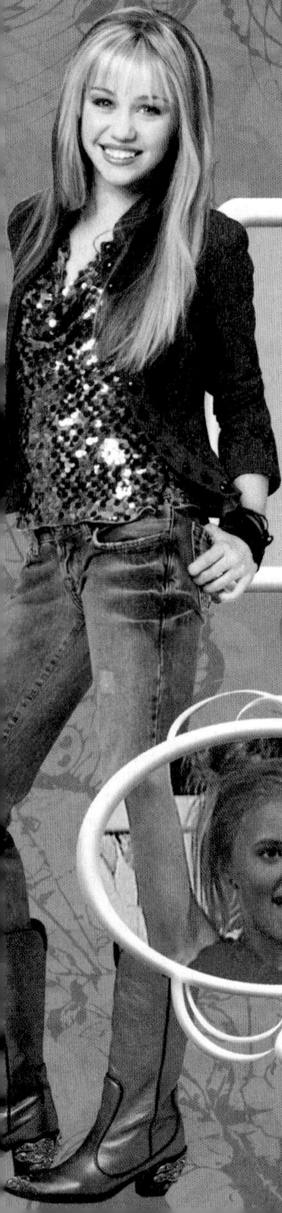

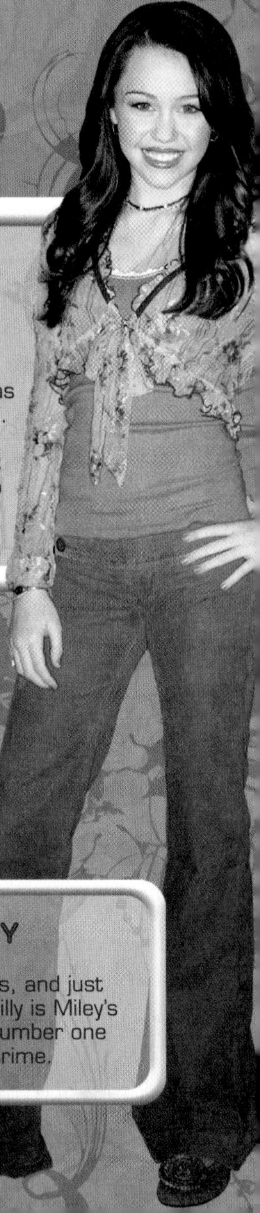

HANNAH MONTANA/ MILEY

She's the girl next door who just so happens to moonlight as a world-famous pop sensation. But underneath the glamour of a superstar, Miley Stewart is a regular girl who gets into all kinds of sticky situations.

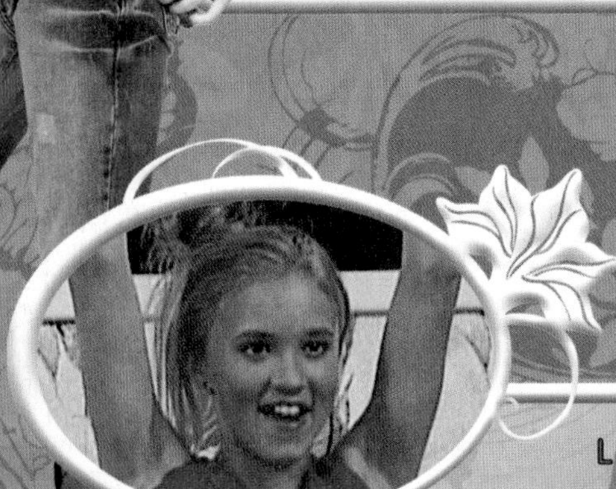

LILLY

Fun, spontaneous, and just a little bit wacky, Lilly is Miley's best friend and number one partner in crime.

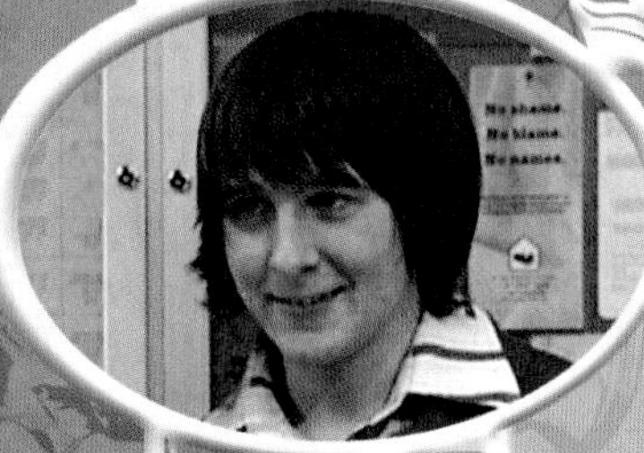

OLIVER

A super-cool goofball, Oliver is a good friend of both Miley and Lilly.

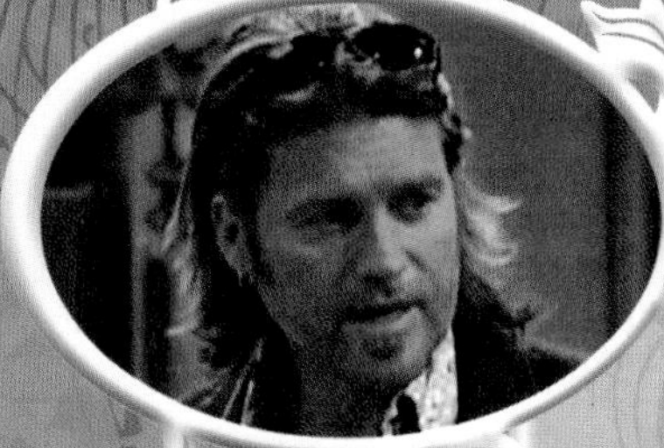

ROBBY

Miley's dad is a country musician who knows enough about showbiz to keep his little girl, the pop star, rock solid.

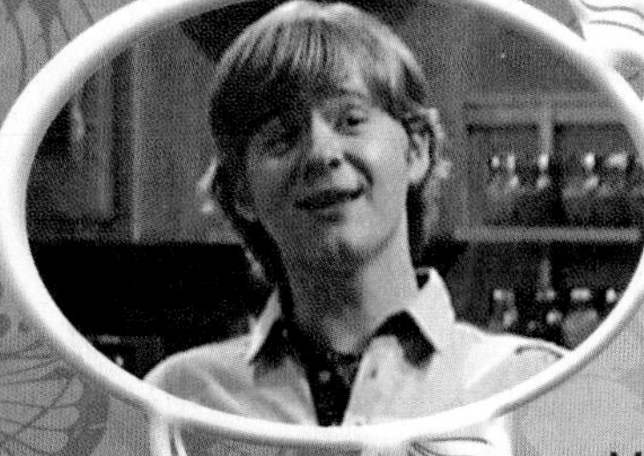

JACKSON

More silly than slick, Miley's brother Jackson definitely has his own way of doing things.

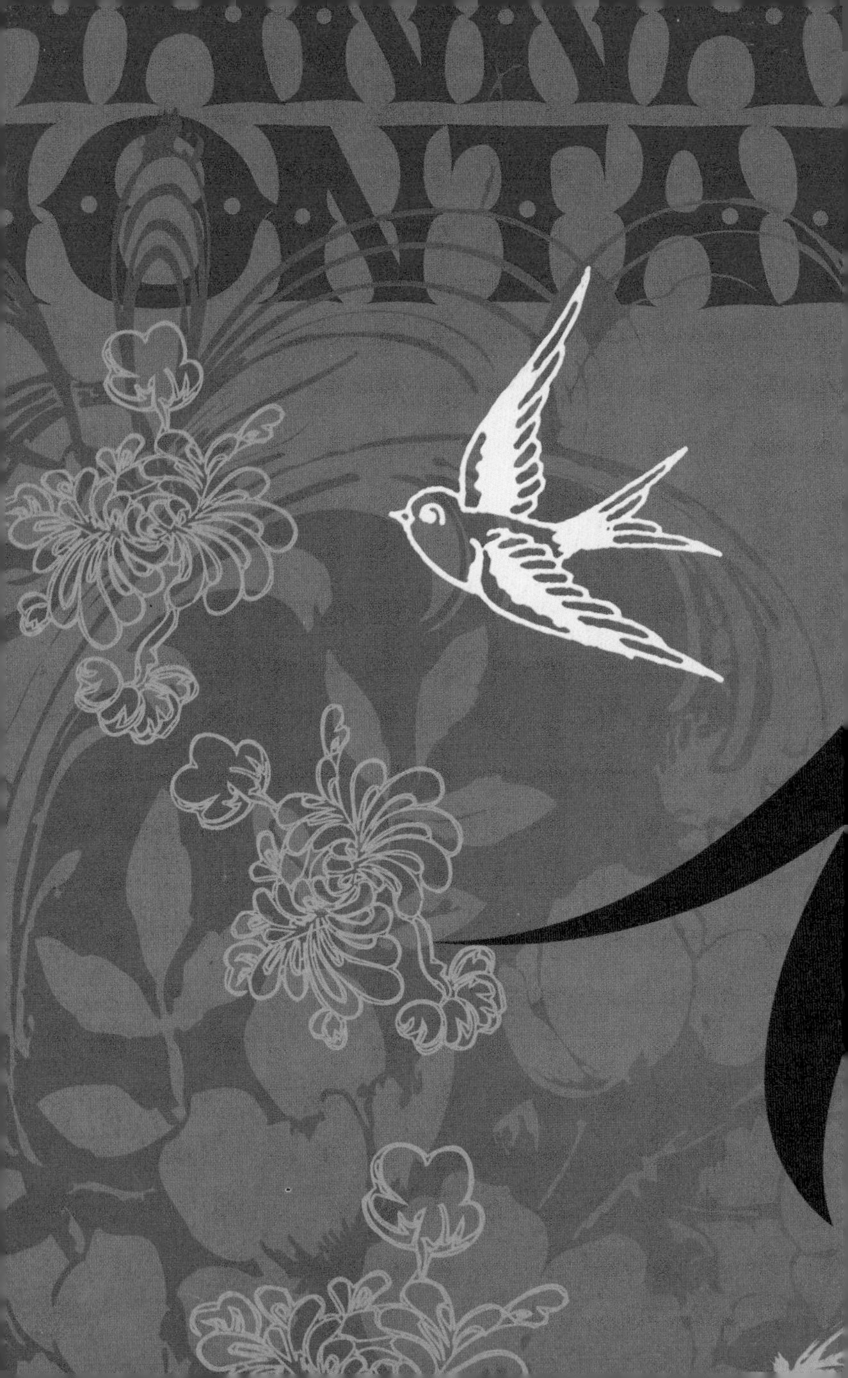

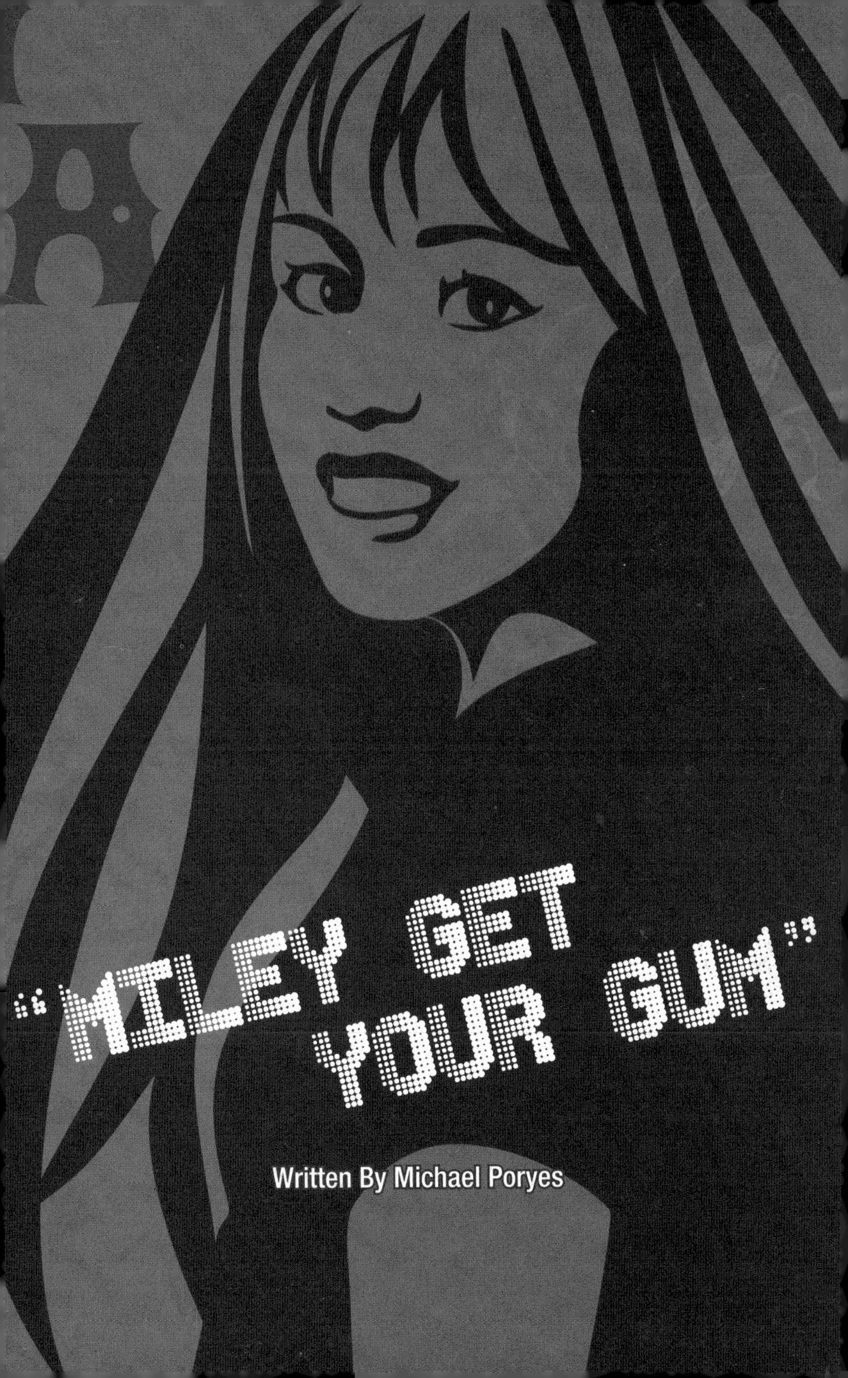

"MILEY GET YOUR GUM"

Written By Michael Poryes

AT THE HANNAH MONTANA CONCERT...

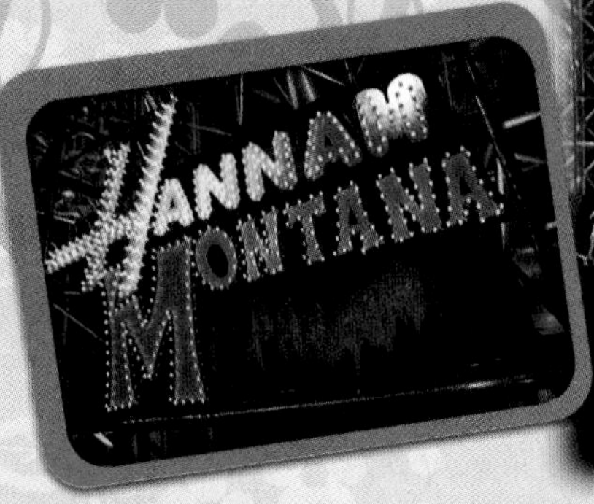
HANNAH MONTANA

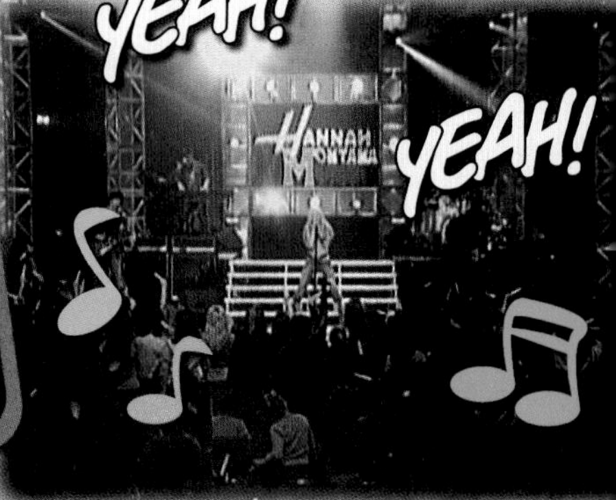
YEAH!
YEAH!

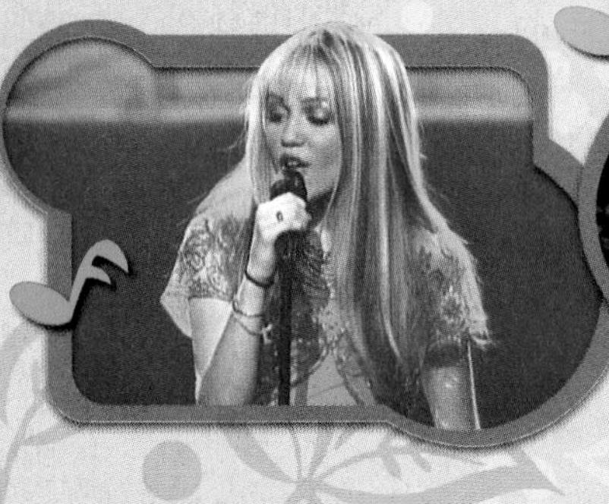

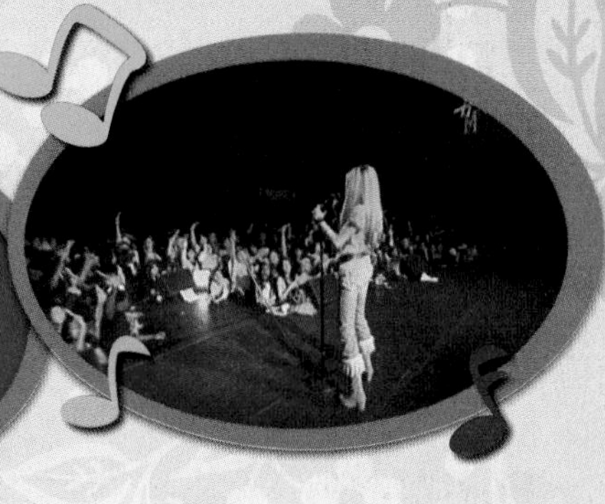

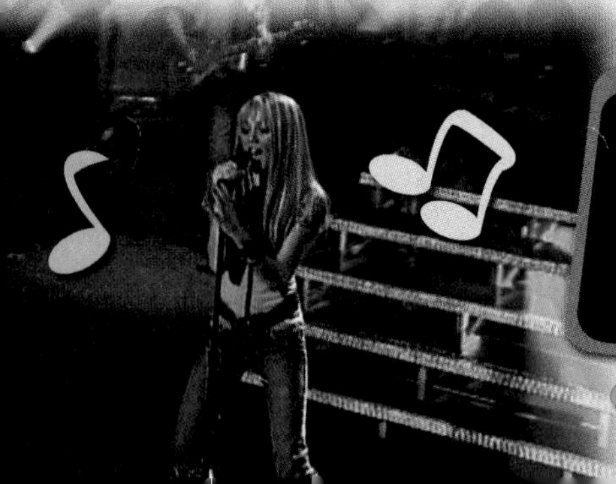

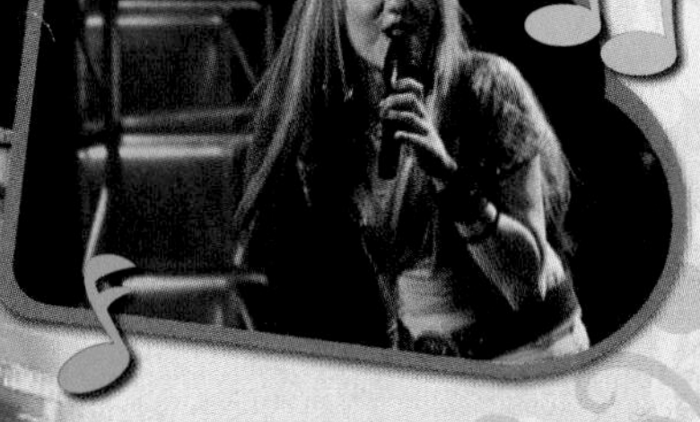

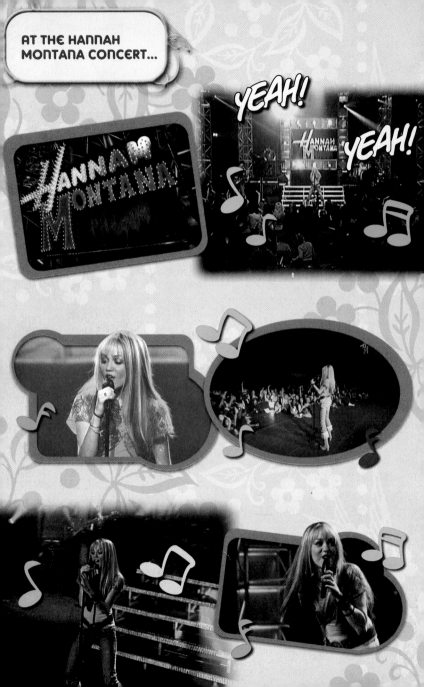

AFTER THE SHOW...

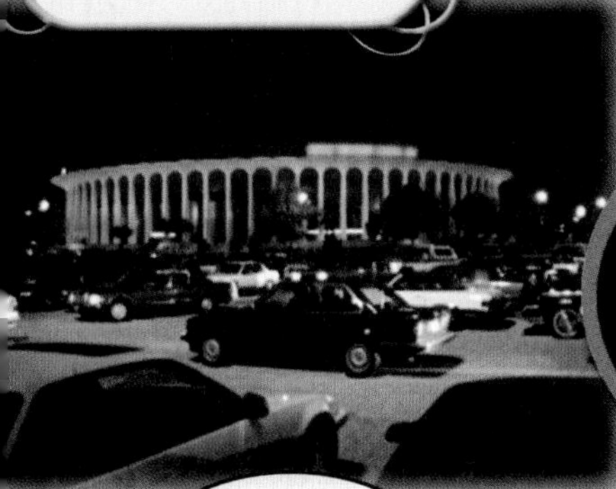

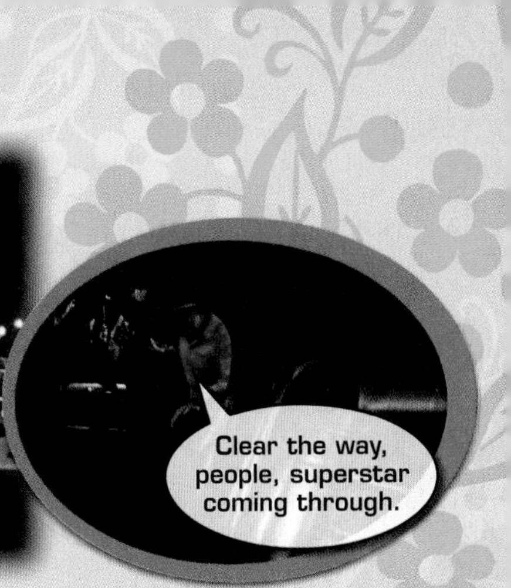
Clear the way, people, superstar coming through.

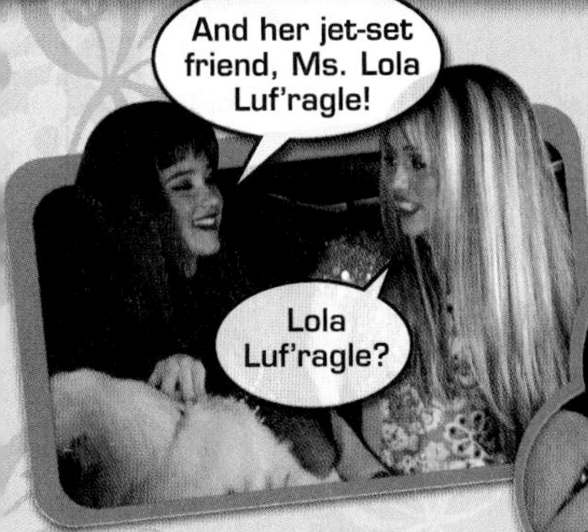
And her jet-set friend, Ms. Lola Luf'ragle!
Lola Luf'ragle?

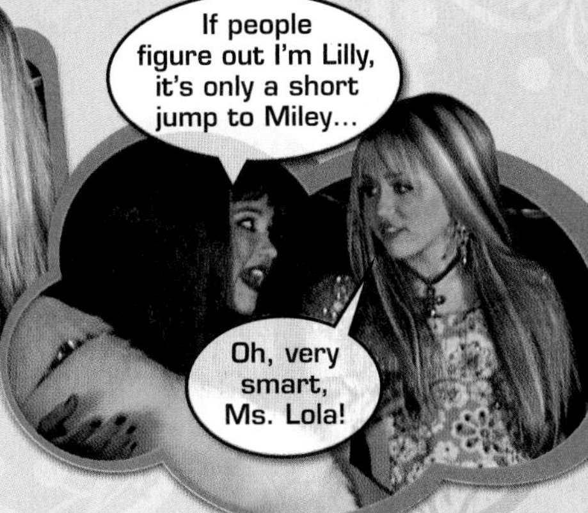
If people figure out I'm Lilly, it's only a short jump to Miley...
Oh, very smart, Ms. Lola!

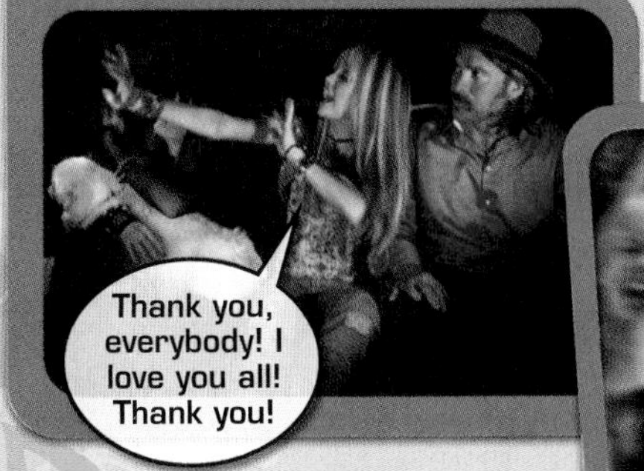
Thank you, everybody! I love you all! Thank you!

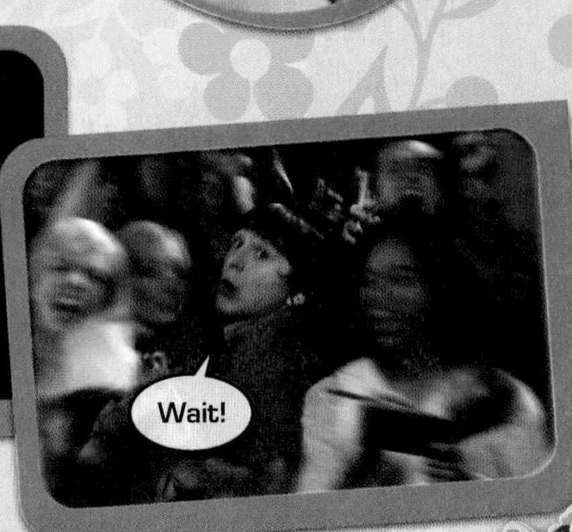
Wait!

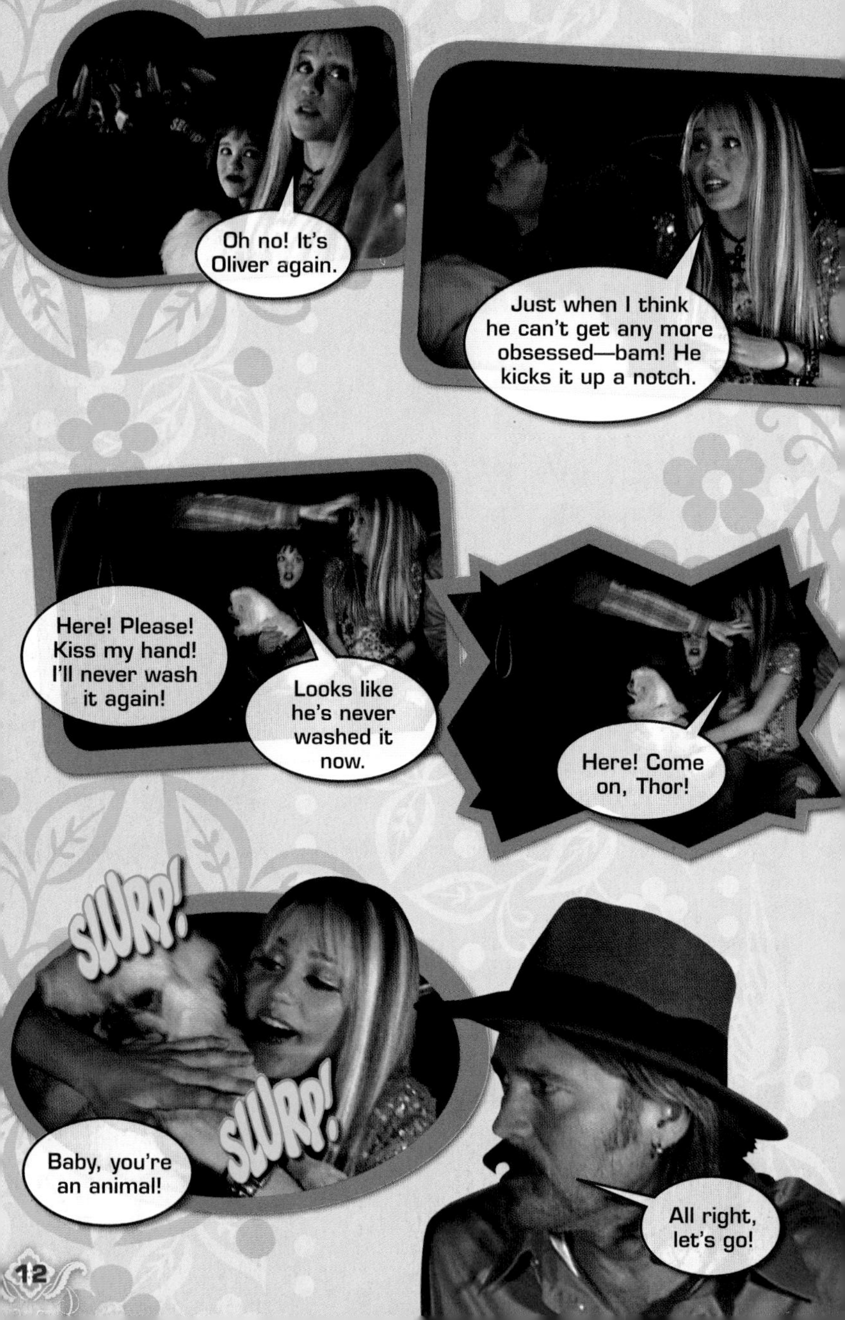
Oh no! It's Oliver again.
Just when I think he can't get any more obsessed—bam! He kicks it up a notch.
Here! Please! Kiss my hand! I'll never wash it again!
Looks like he's never washed it now.
Here! Come on, Thor!
SLURP!
SLURP!
Baby, you're an animal!
All right, let's go!

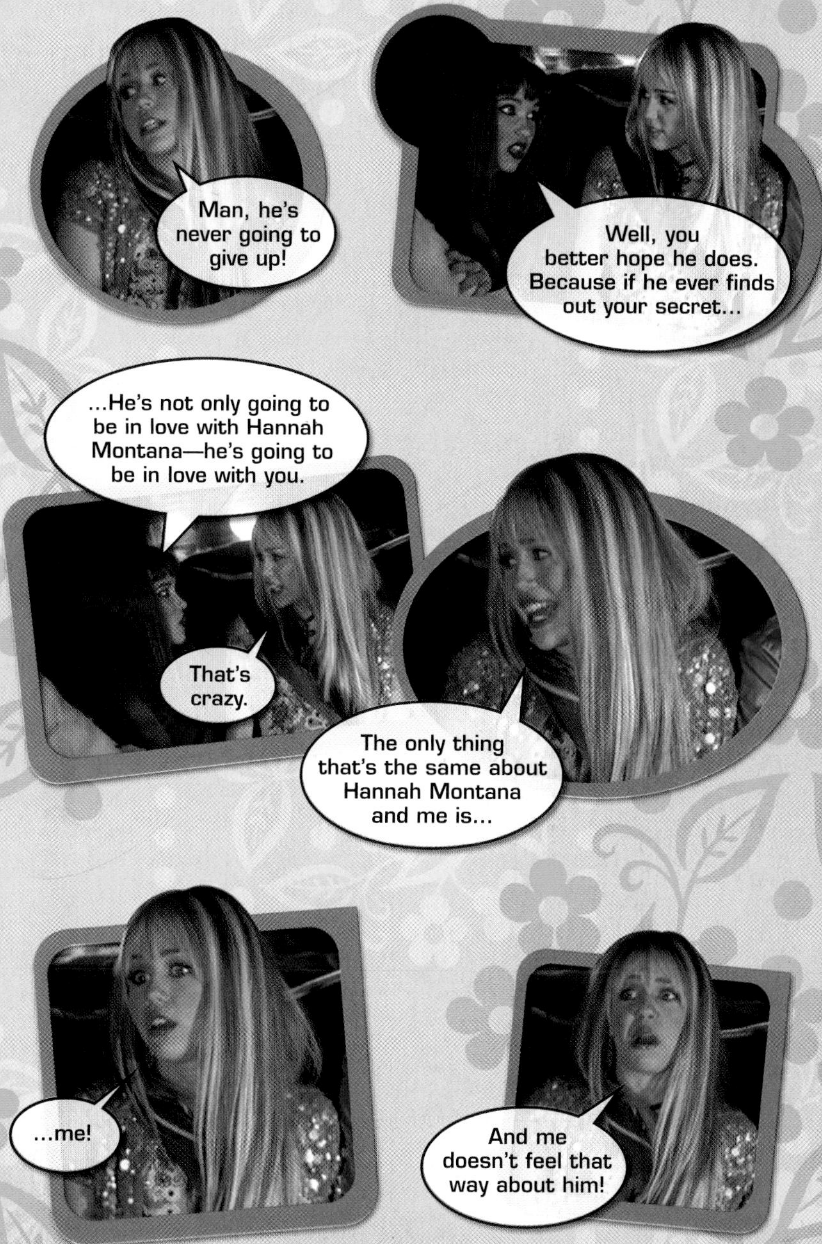
Man, he's never going to give up!
Well, you better hope he does. Because if he ever finds out your secret...
...He's not only going to be in love with Hannah Montana—he's going to be in love with you.
That's crazy.
The only thing that's the same about Hannah Montana and me is...
...me!
And me doesn't feel that way about him!

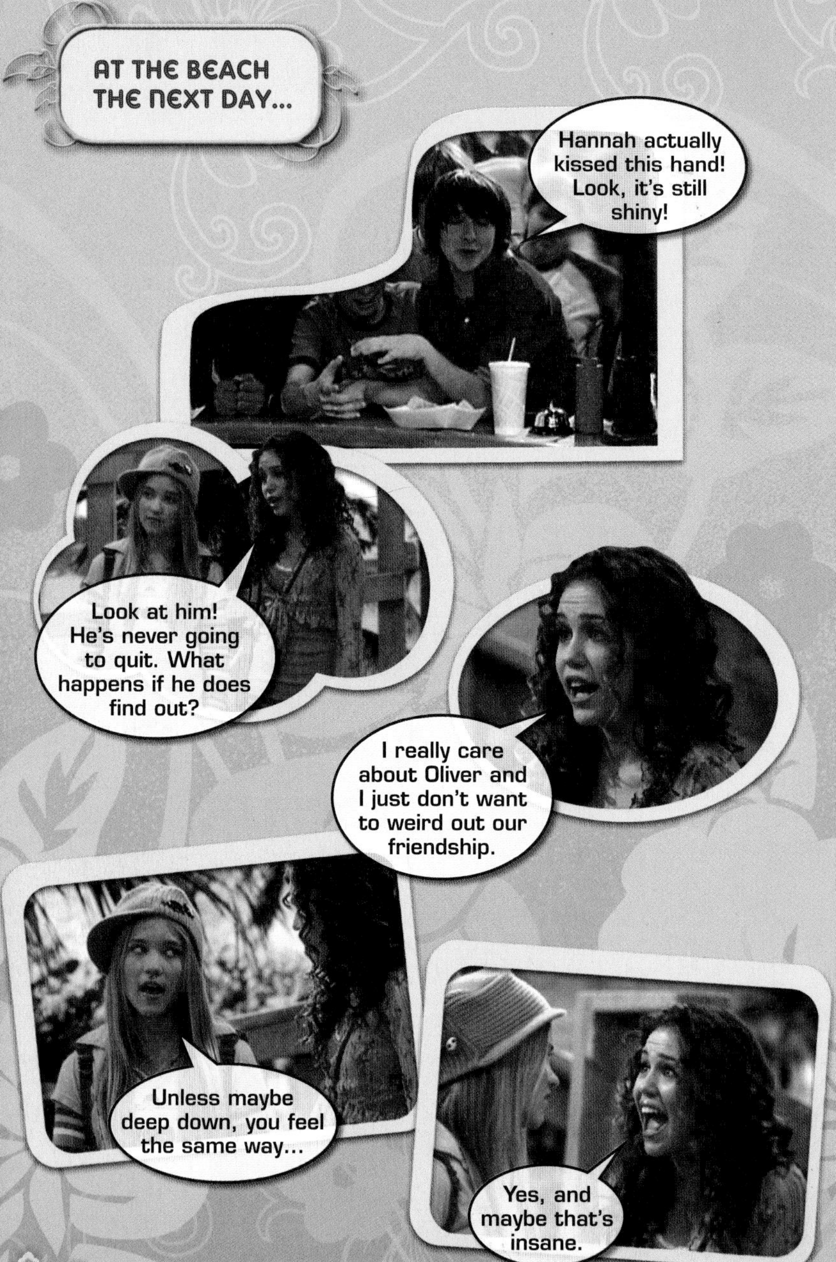
AT THE BEACH THE NEXT DAY...
Hannah actually kissed this hand! Look, it's still shiny!
Look at him! He's never going to quit. What happens if he does find out?
I really care about Oliver and I just don't want to weird out our friendship.
Unless maybe deep down, you feel the same way...
Yes, and maybe that's insane.

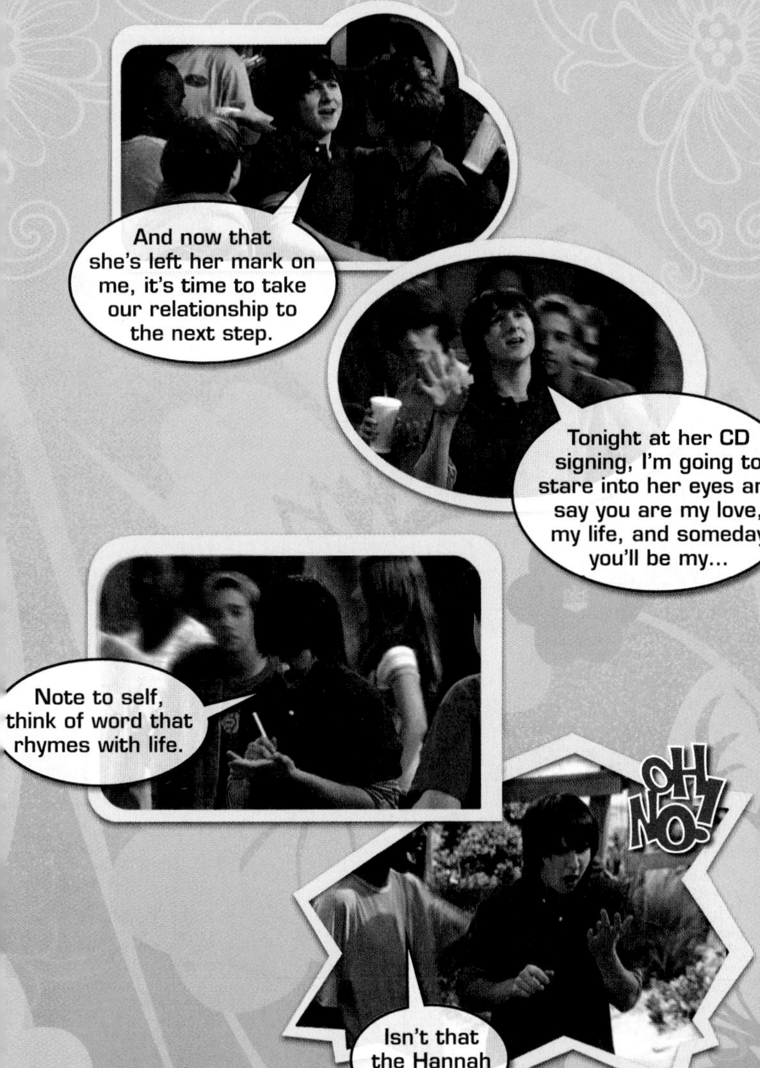
And now that she's left her mark on me, it's time to take our relationship to the next step.
Tonight at her CD signing, I'm going to stare into her eyes and say you are my love, my life, and someday you'll be my...
Note to self, think of word that rhymes with life.
OH NO!
Isn't that the Hannah hand?

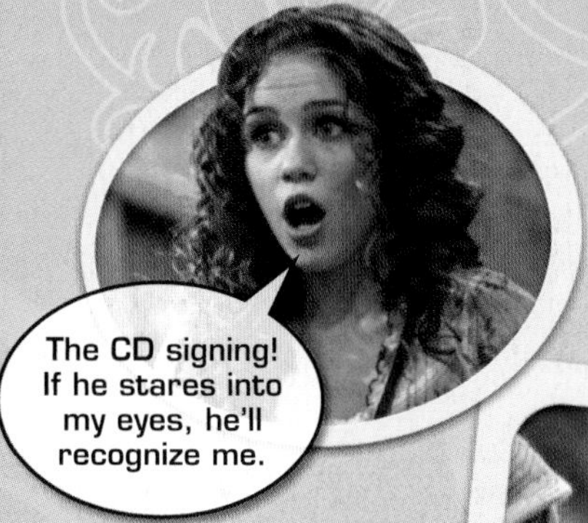
The CD signing! If he stares into my eyes, he'll recognize me.

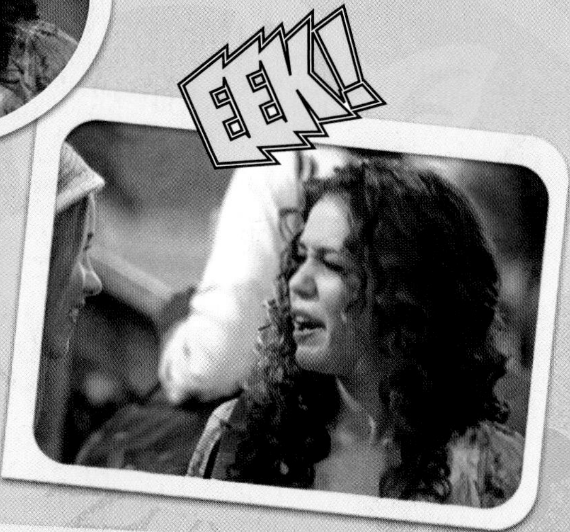
EEK!

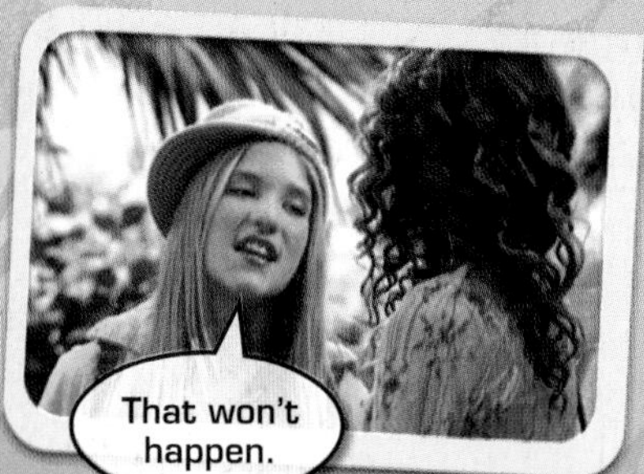
That won't happen.

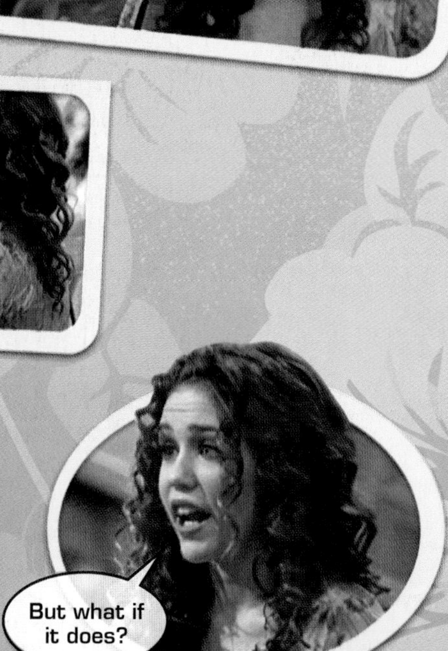
But what if it does?

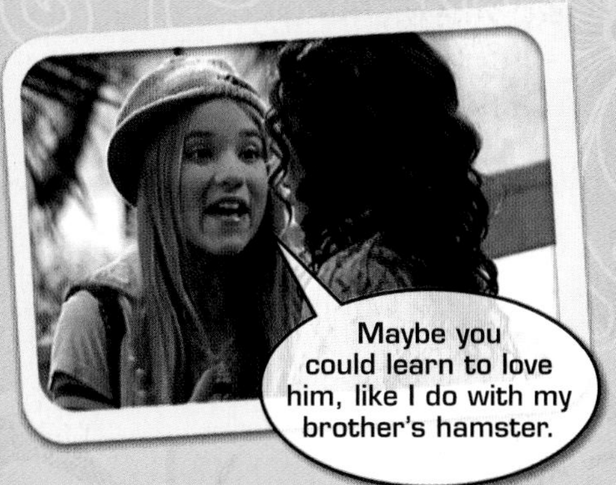
Maybe you could learn to love him, like I do with my brother's hamster.

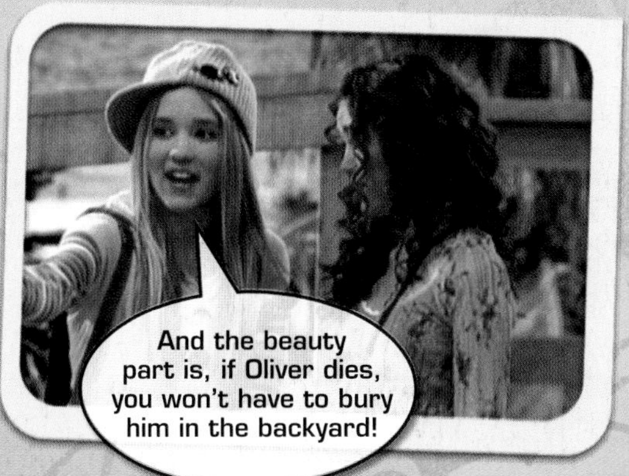
And the beauty part is, if Oliver dies, you won't have to bury him in the backyard!

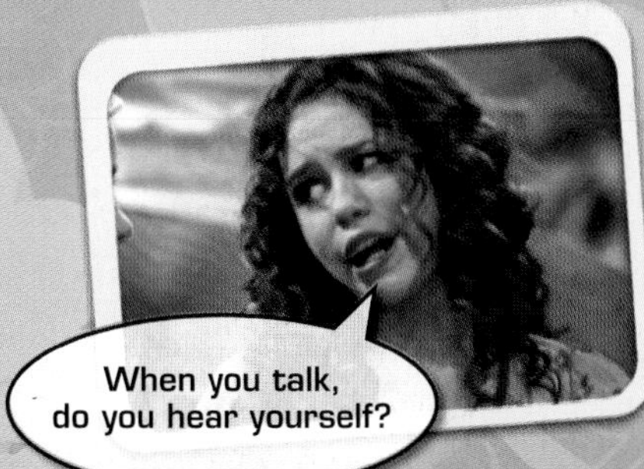
When you talk, do you hear yourself?

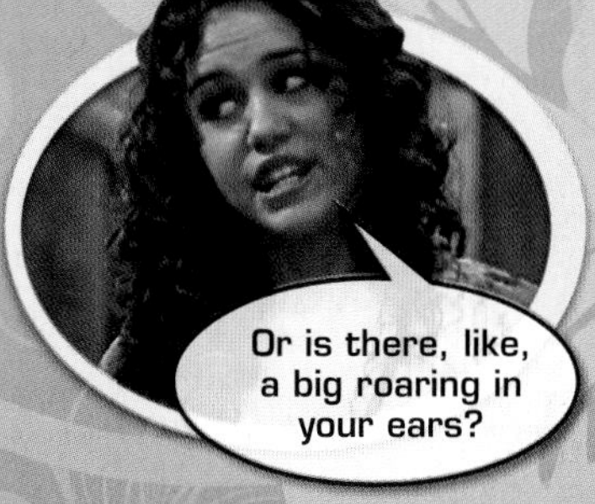
Or is there, like, a big roaring in your ears?

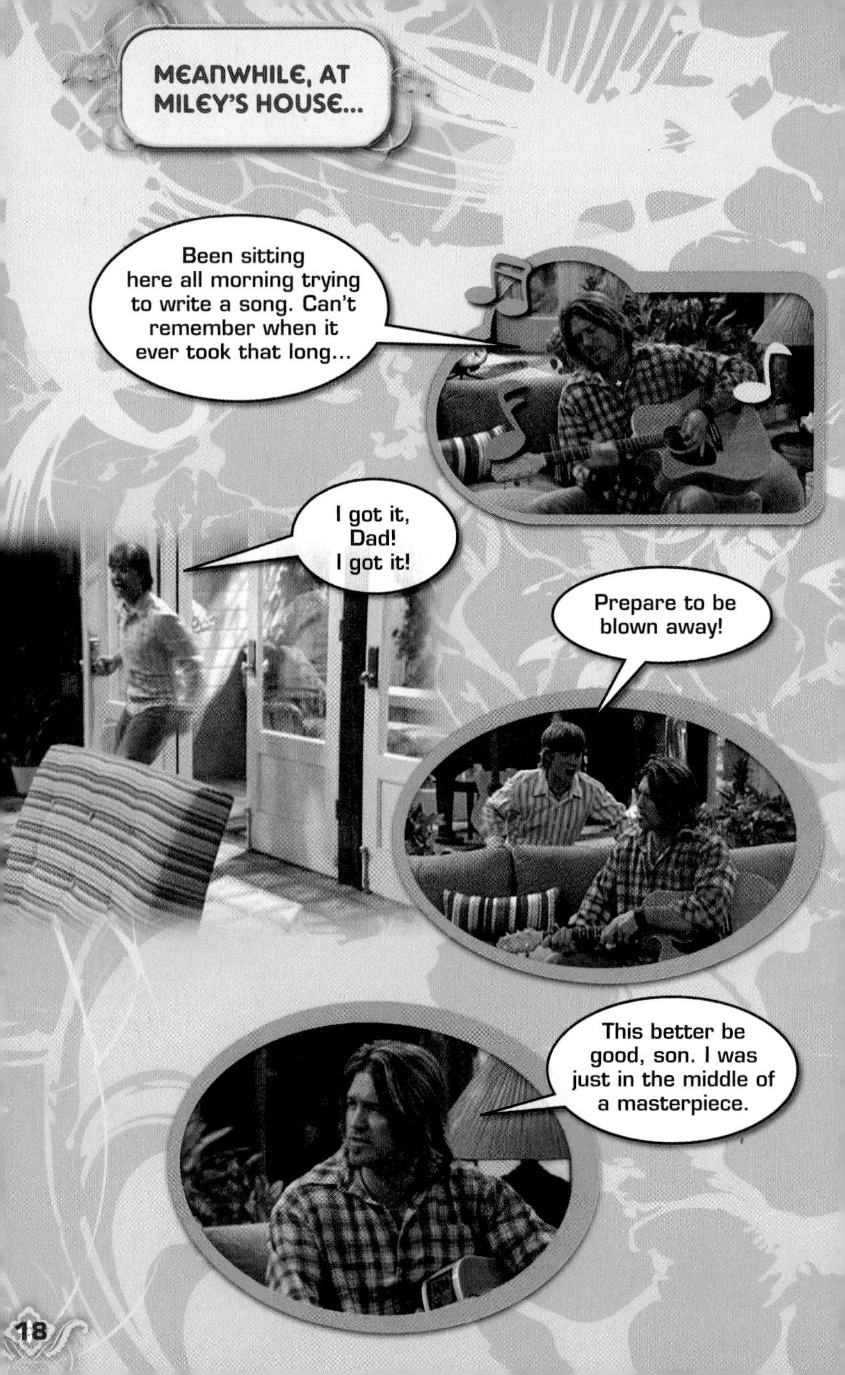
MEANWHILE, AT MILEY'S HOUSE...
Been sitting here all morning trying to write a song. Can't remember when it ever took that long...
I got it, Dad! I got it!
Prepare to be blown away!
This better be good, son. I was just in the middle of a masterpiece.

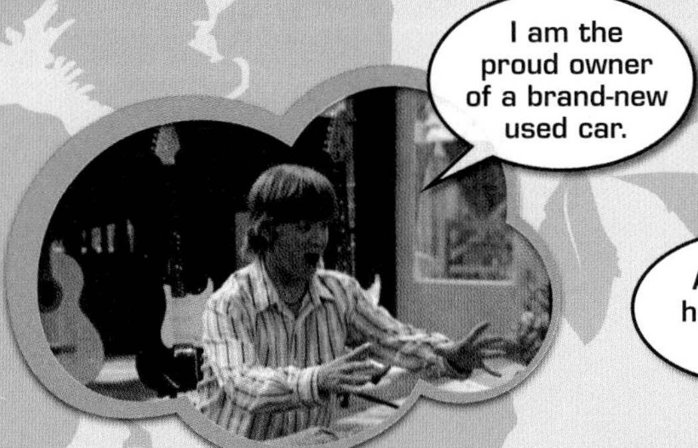
I am the proud owner of a brand-new used car.
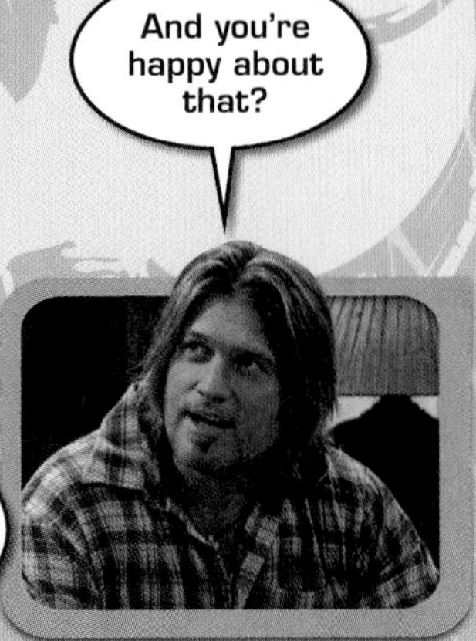
And you're happy about that?
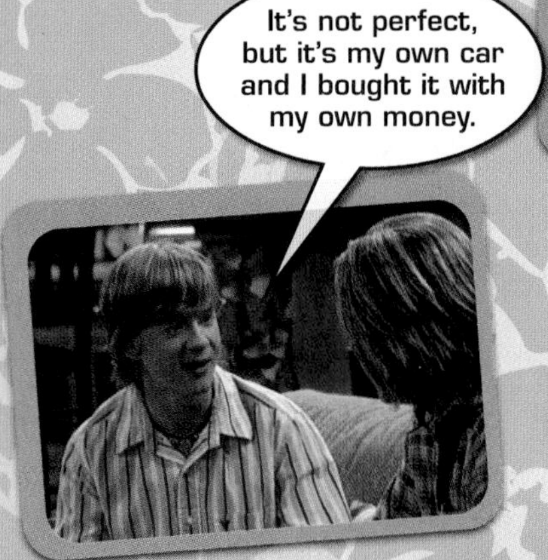
It's not perfect, but it's my own car and I bought it with my own money.
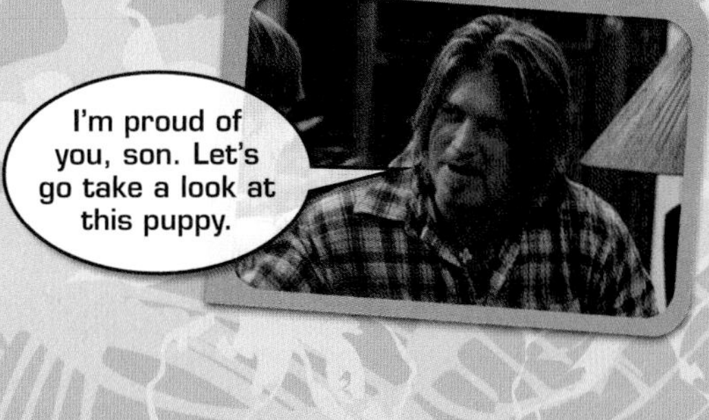
I'm proud of you, son. Let's go take a look at this puppy.

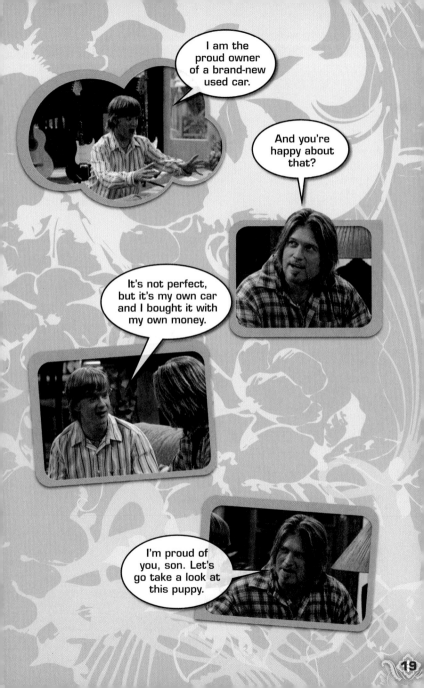

MOMENTS LATER...

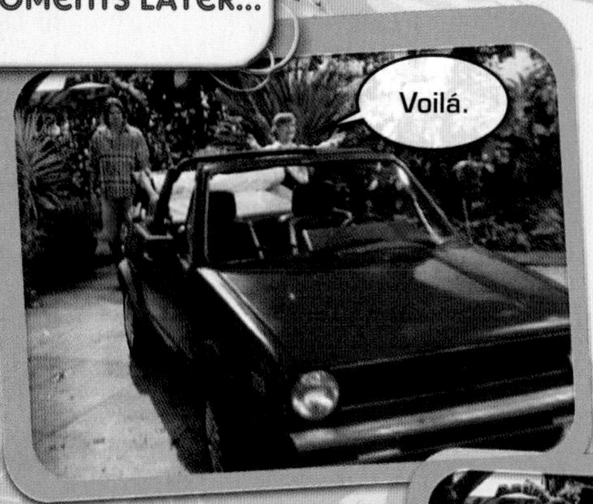
Voilá.

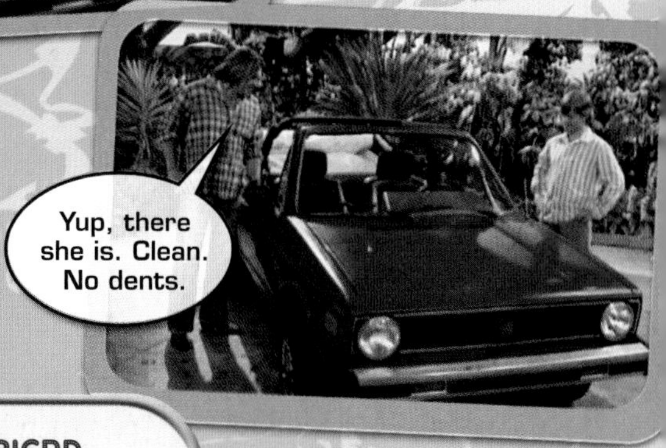
Yup, there she is. Clean. No dents.

WHEN JACKSON'S FRIEND, COOPER, SEES THE CAR, HE TELLS JACKSON ONLY GIRLS DRIVE THIS THING. IT'S A CHICK-MOBILE!

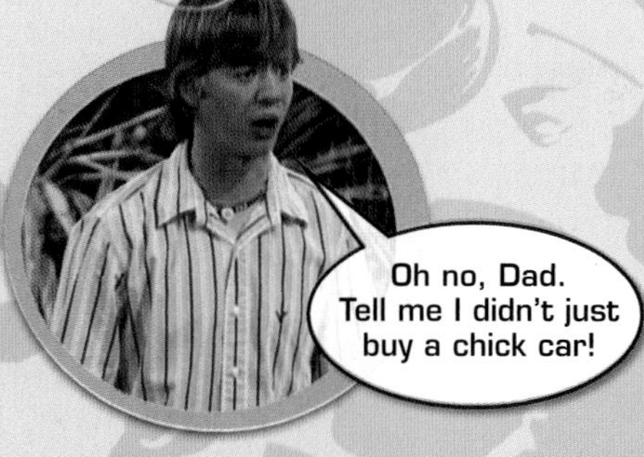
Oh no, Dad. Tell me I didn't just buy a chick car!

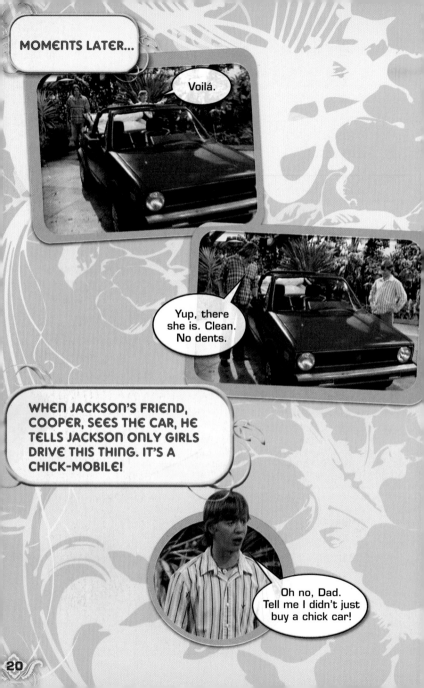

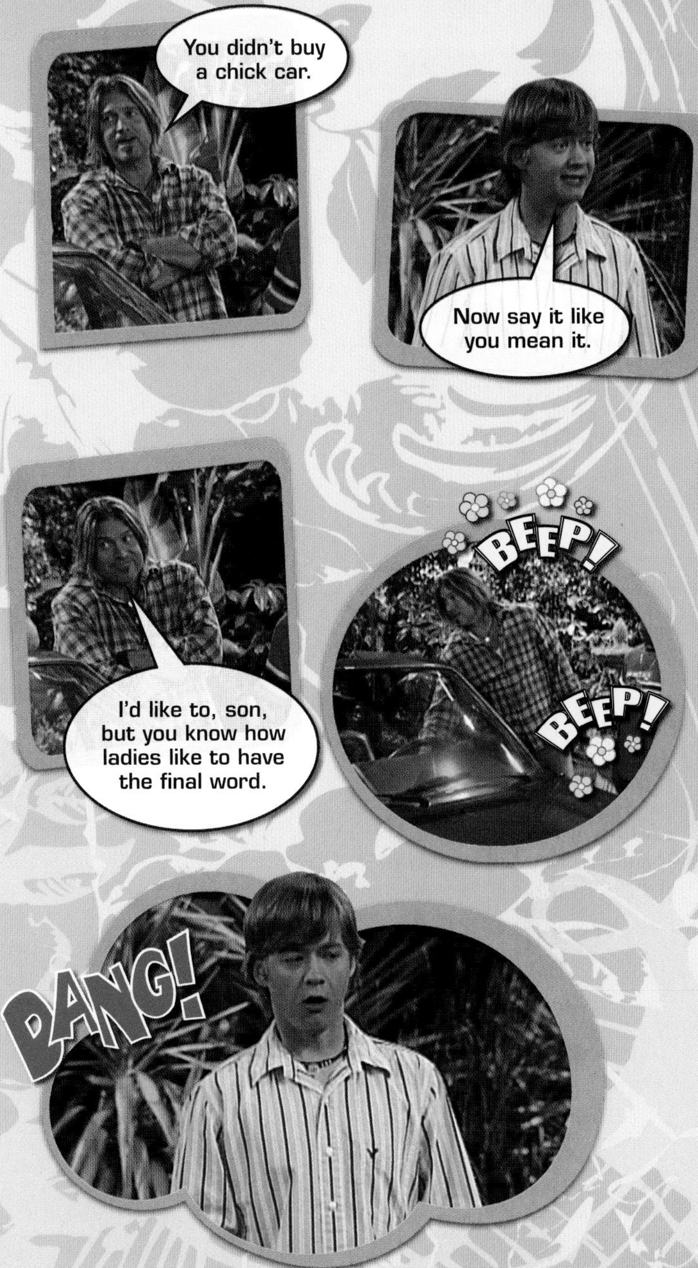
You didn't buy a chick car.
Now say it like you mean it.
I'd like to, son, but you know how ladies like to have the final word.
BEEP!
BEEP!
BANG!

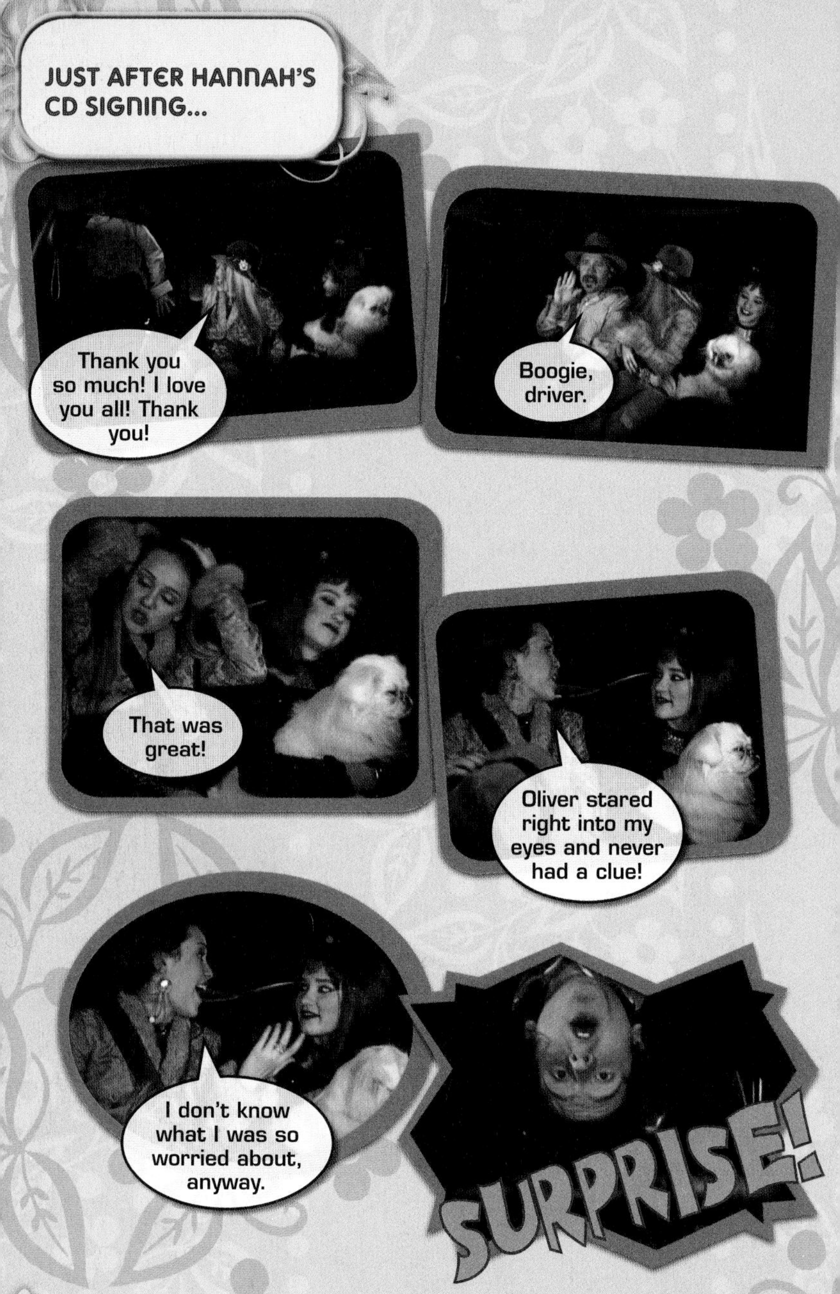
JUST AFTER HANNAH'S CD SIGNING...
Thank you so much! I love you all! Thank you!
Boogie, driver.
That was great!
Oliver stared right into my eyes and never had a clue!
I don't know what I was so worried about, anyway.
SURPRISE!

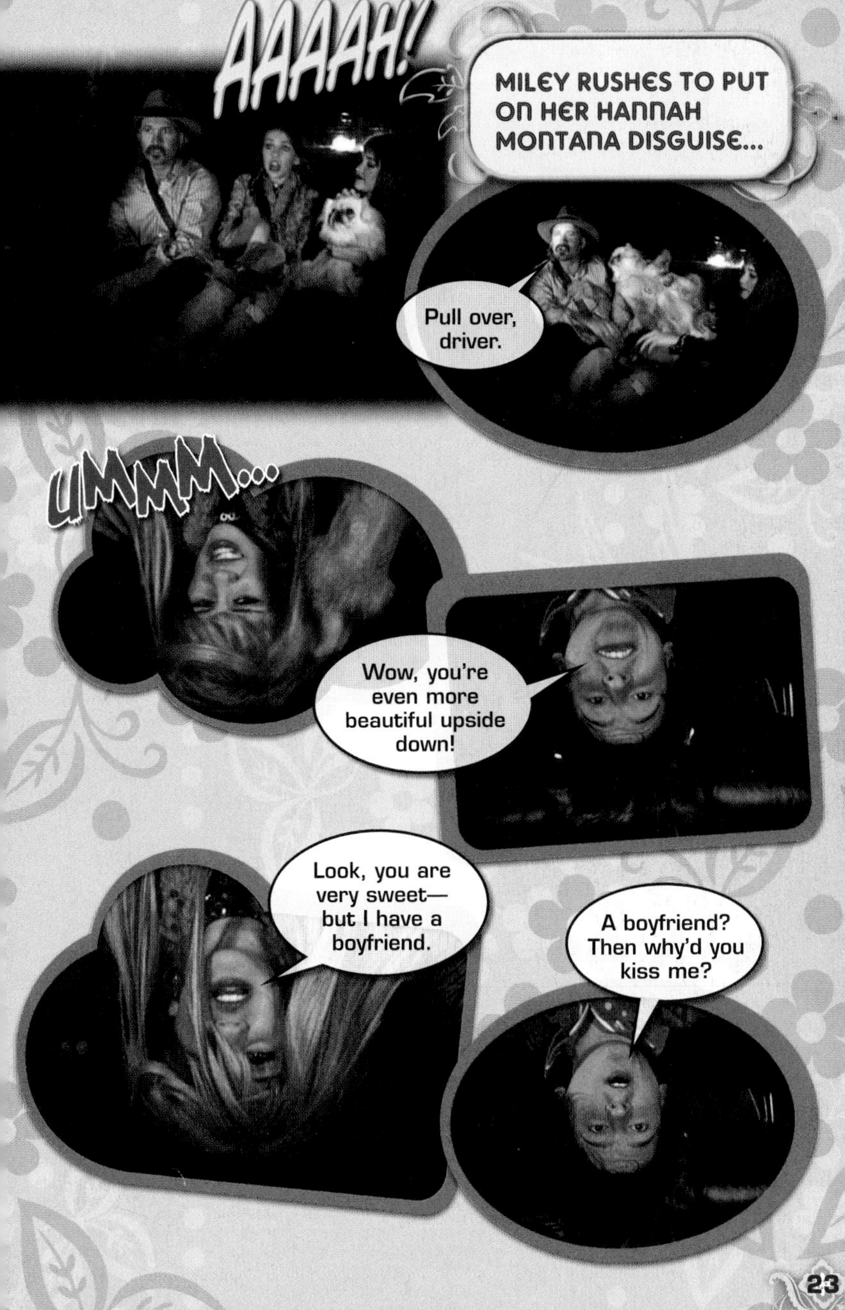
AAAAH!
MILEY RUSHES TO PUT ON HER HANNAH MONTANA DISGUISE...
Pull over, driver.
UMMM...
Wow, you're even more beautiful upside down!
Look, you are very sweet—but I have a boyfriend.
A boyfriend? Then why'd you kiss me?

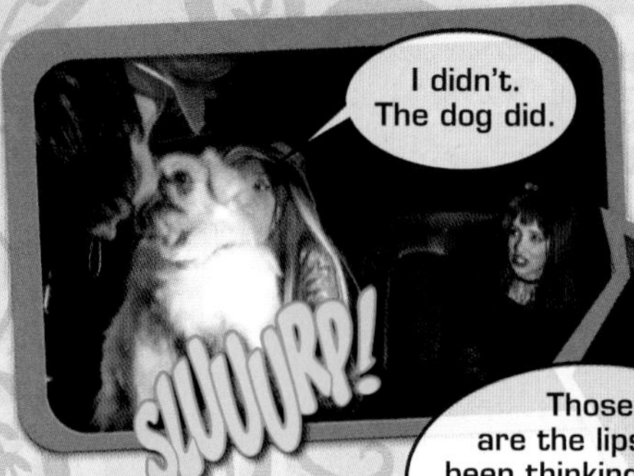
I didn't. The dog did.
SLUUURP!

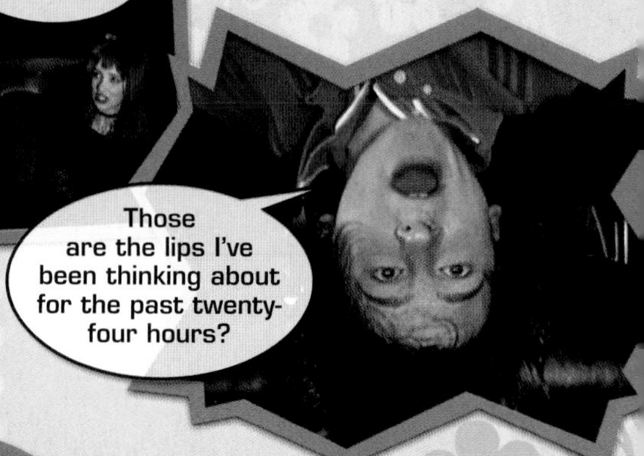
Those are the lips I've been thinking about for the past twenty-four hours?

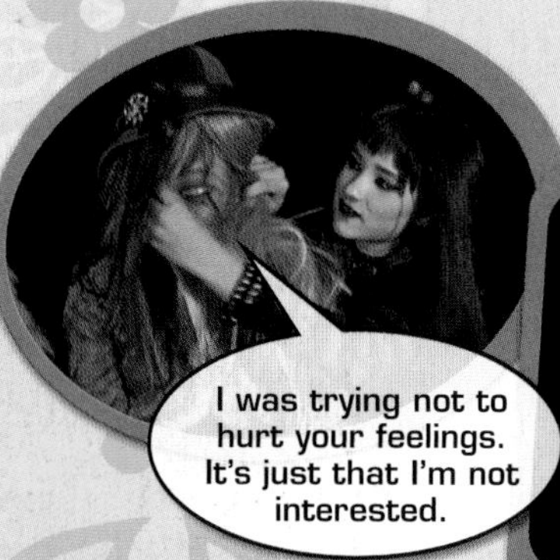
I was trying not to hurt your feelings. It's just that I'm not interested.

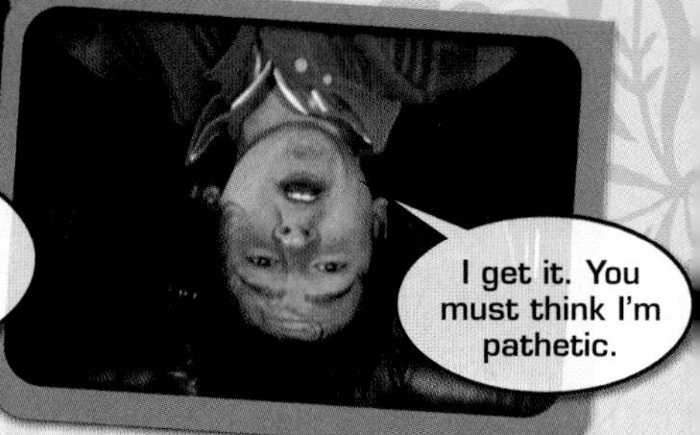
I get it. You must think I'm pathetic.

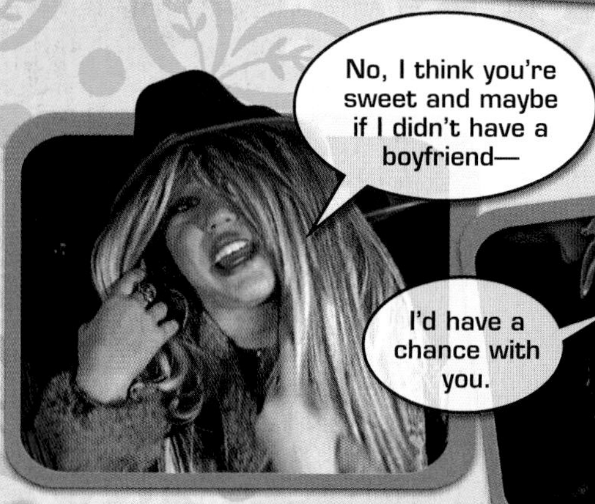
No, I think you're sweet and maybe if I didn't have a boyfriend—

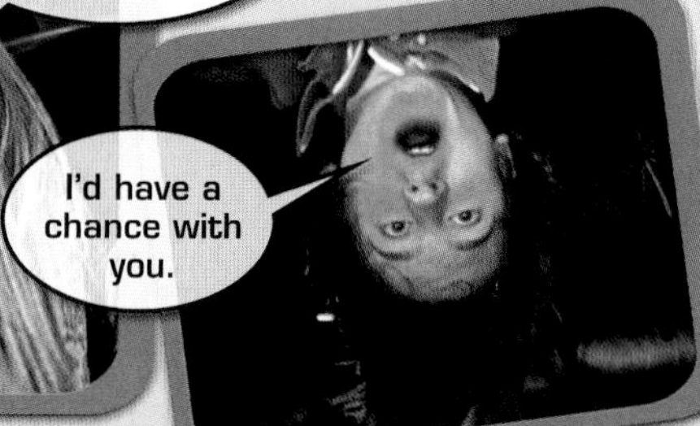
I'd have a chance with you.

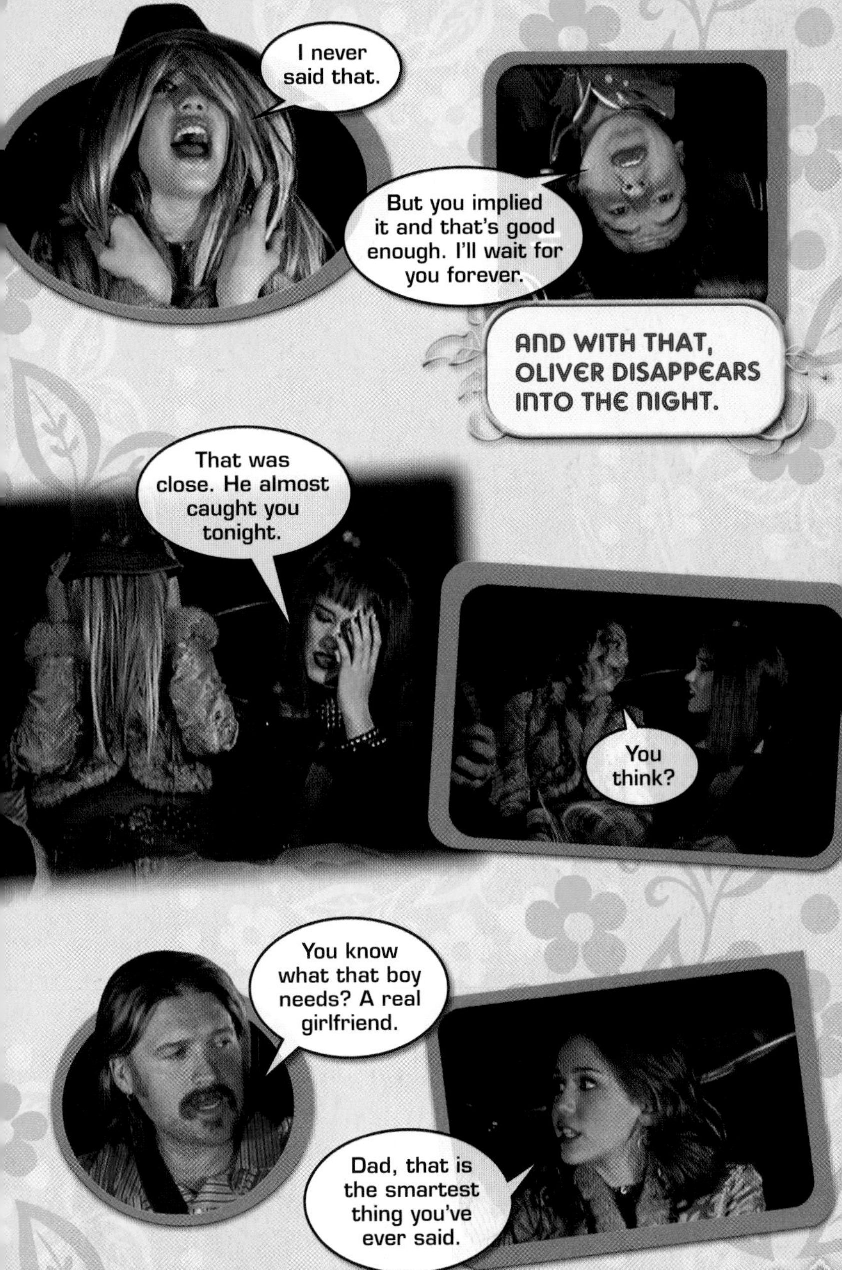
I never said that.
But you implied it and that's good enough. I'll wait for you forever.
AND WITH THAT, OLIVER DISAPPEARS INTO THE NIGHT.
That was close. He almost caught you tonight.
You think?
You know what that boy needs? A real girlfriend.
Dad, that is the smartest thing you've ever said.

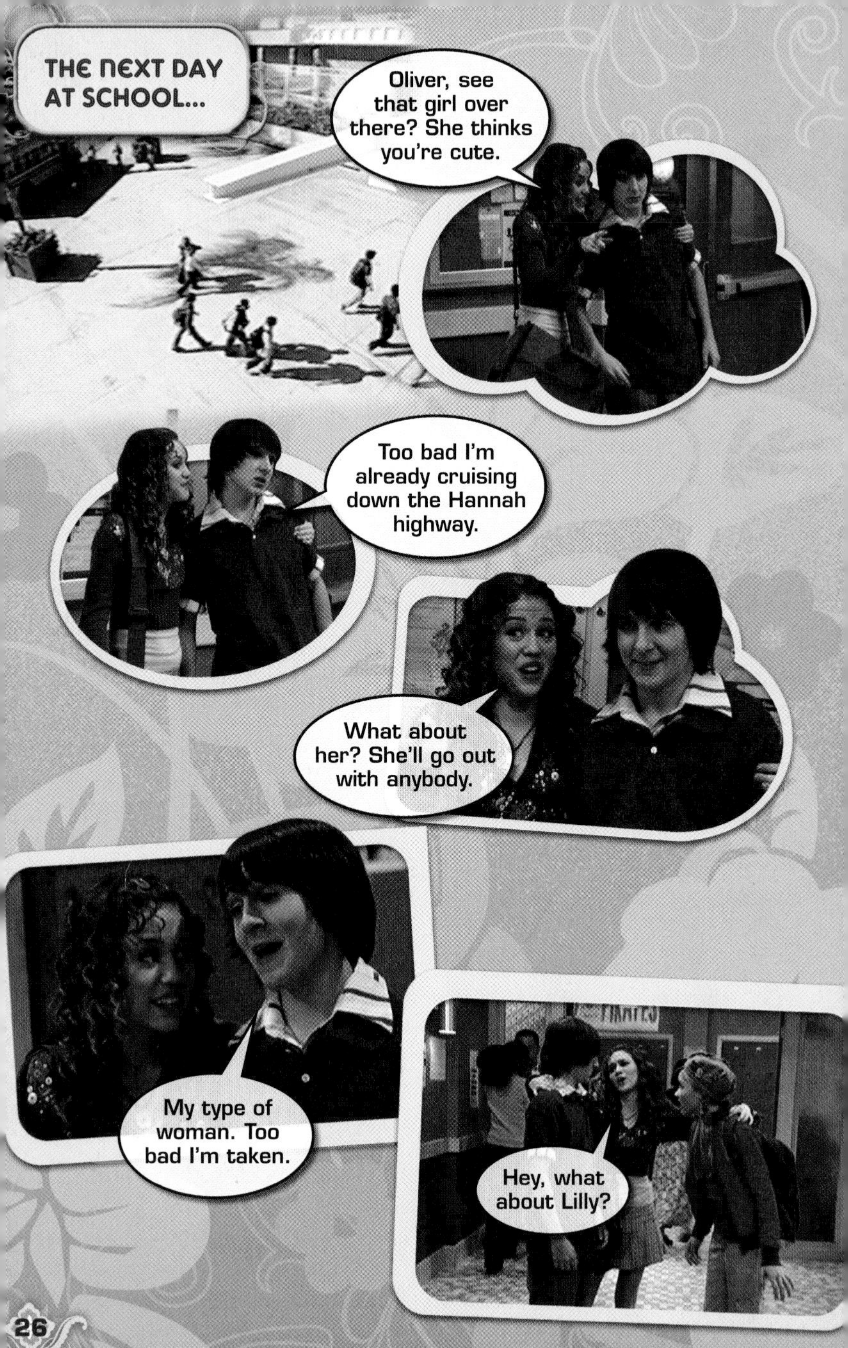
THE NEXT DAY AT SCHOOL...
Oliver, see that girl over there? She thinks you're cute.
Too bad I'm already cruising down the Hannah highway.
What about her? She'll go out with anybody.
My type of woman. Too bad I'm taken.
Hey, what about Lilly?

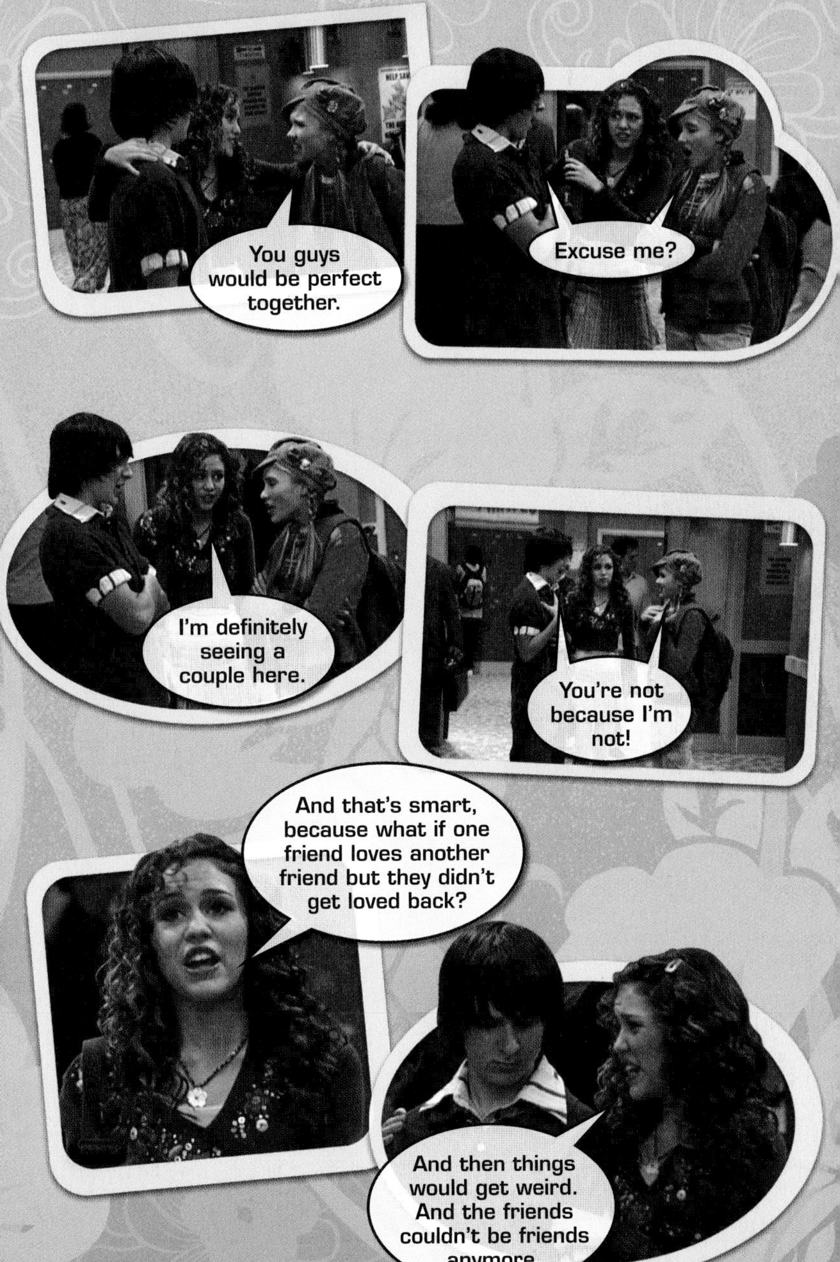
You guys would be perfect together.
Excuse me?
I'm definitely seeing a couple here.
You're not because I'm not!
And that's smart, because what if one friend loves another friend but they didn't get loved back?
And then things would get weird. And the friends couldn't be friends anymore.

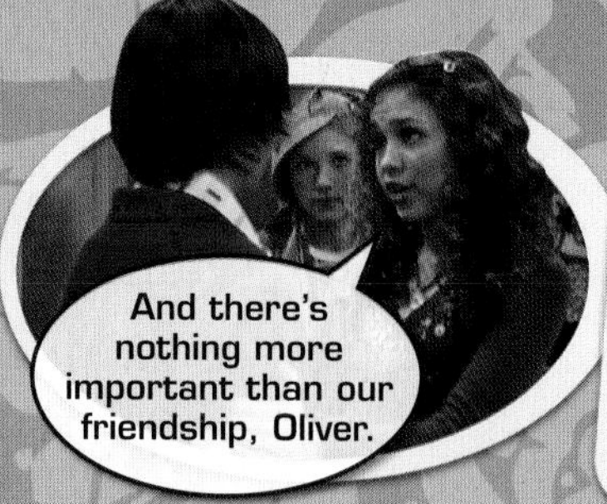
And there's nothing more important than our friendship, Oliver.
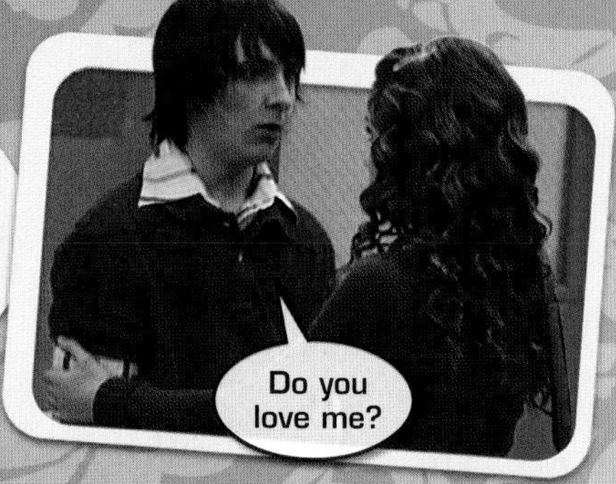
Do you love me?
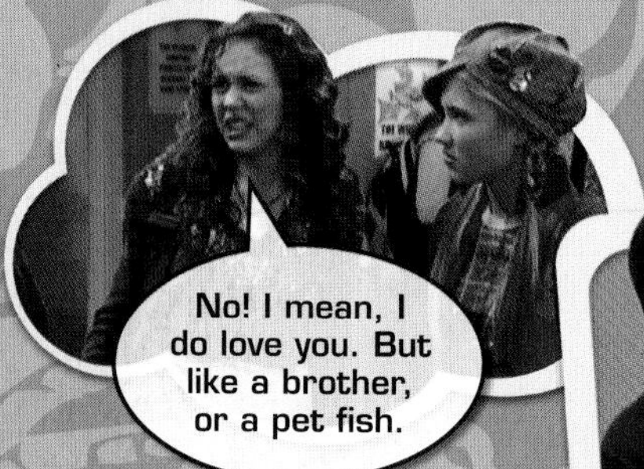
No! I mean, I do love you. But like a brother, or a pet fish.
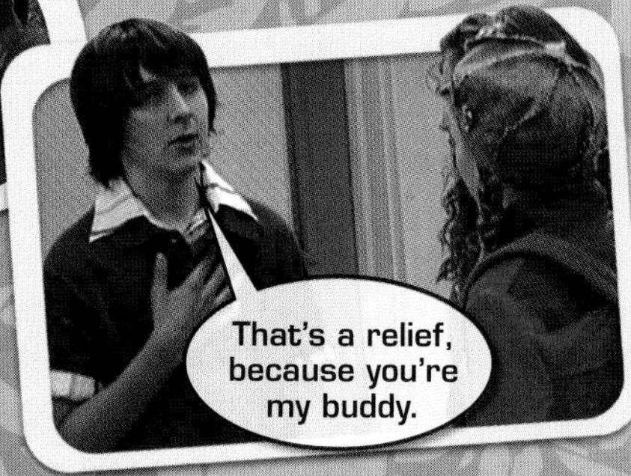
That's a relief, because you're my buddy.
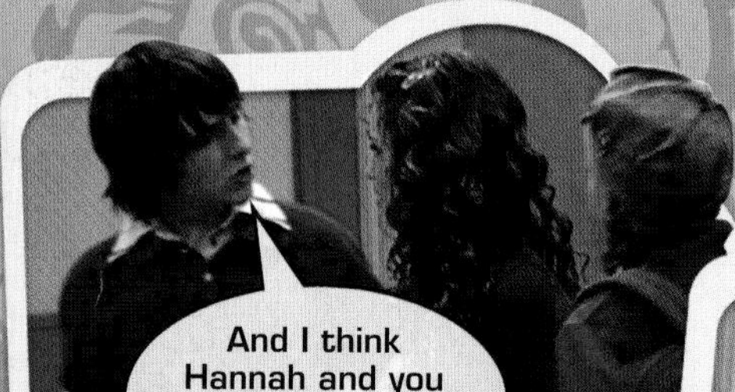
And I think Hannah and you could wind up being close friends.
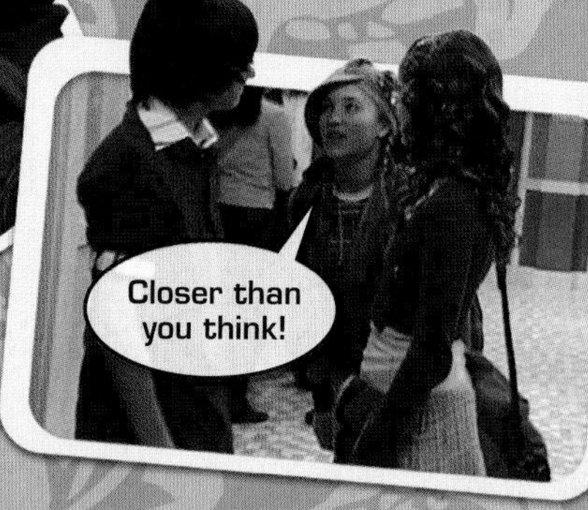
Closer than you think!

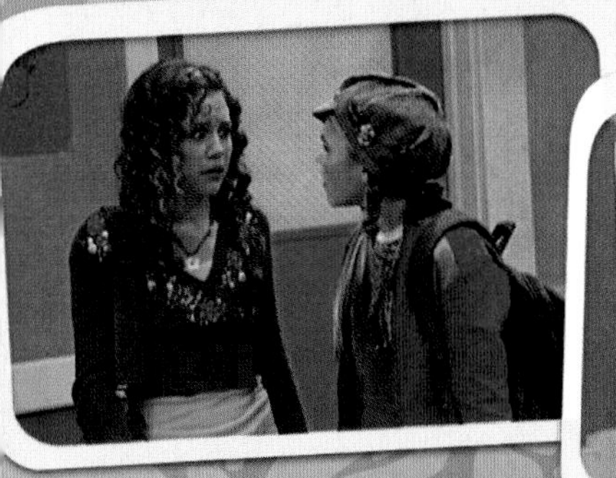

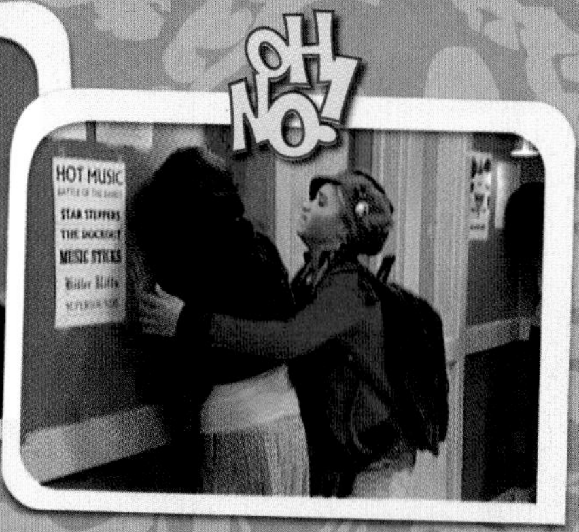
OH NO!
HOT MUSIC

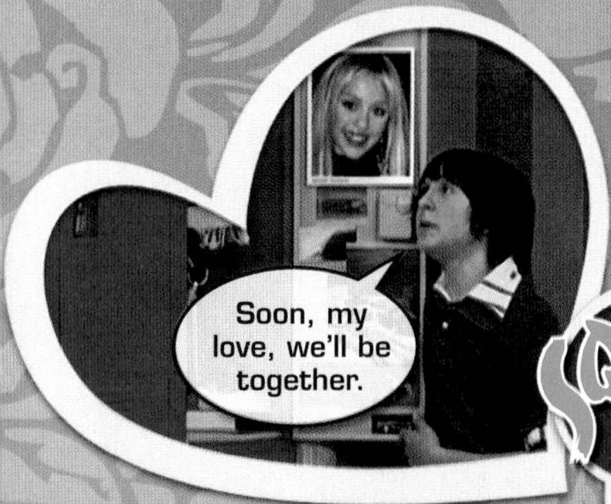
Soon, my love, we'll be together.

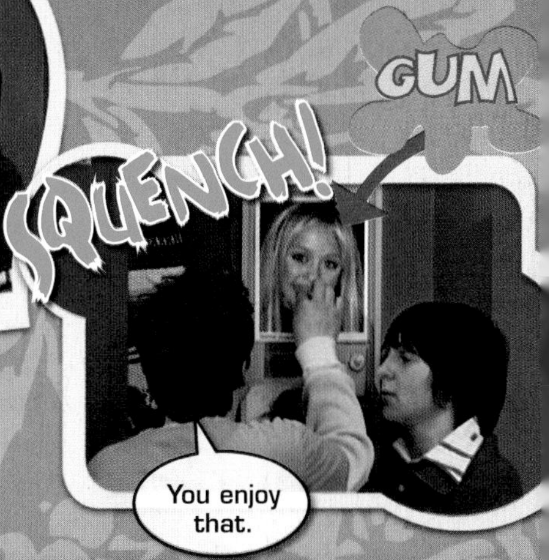
GUM
SQUENCH!
You enjoy that.

OLIVER IS FURIOUS BECAUSE HE HATES GUM.

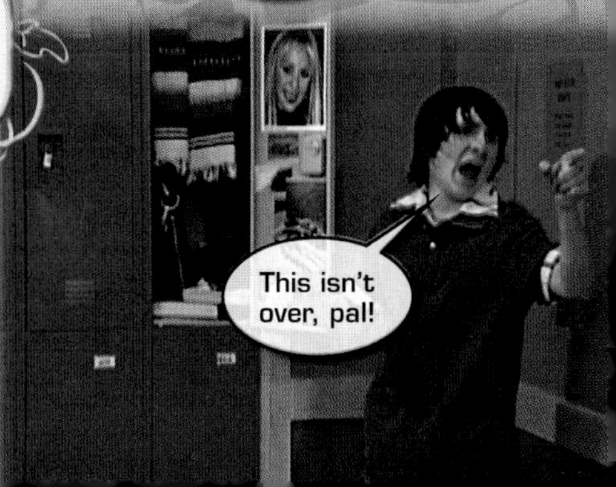
This isn't over, pal!

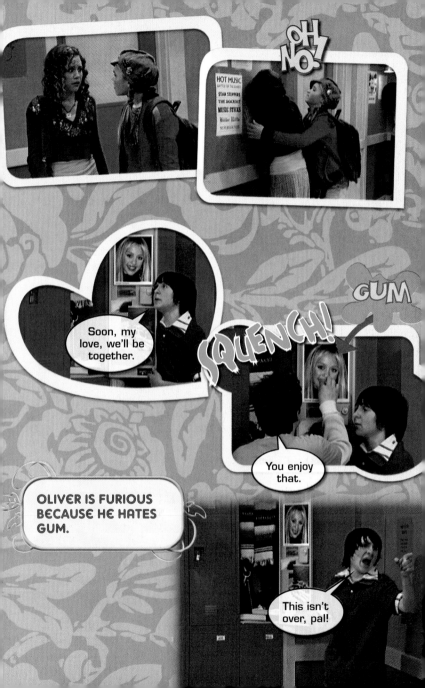

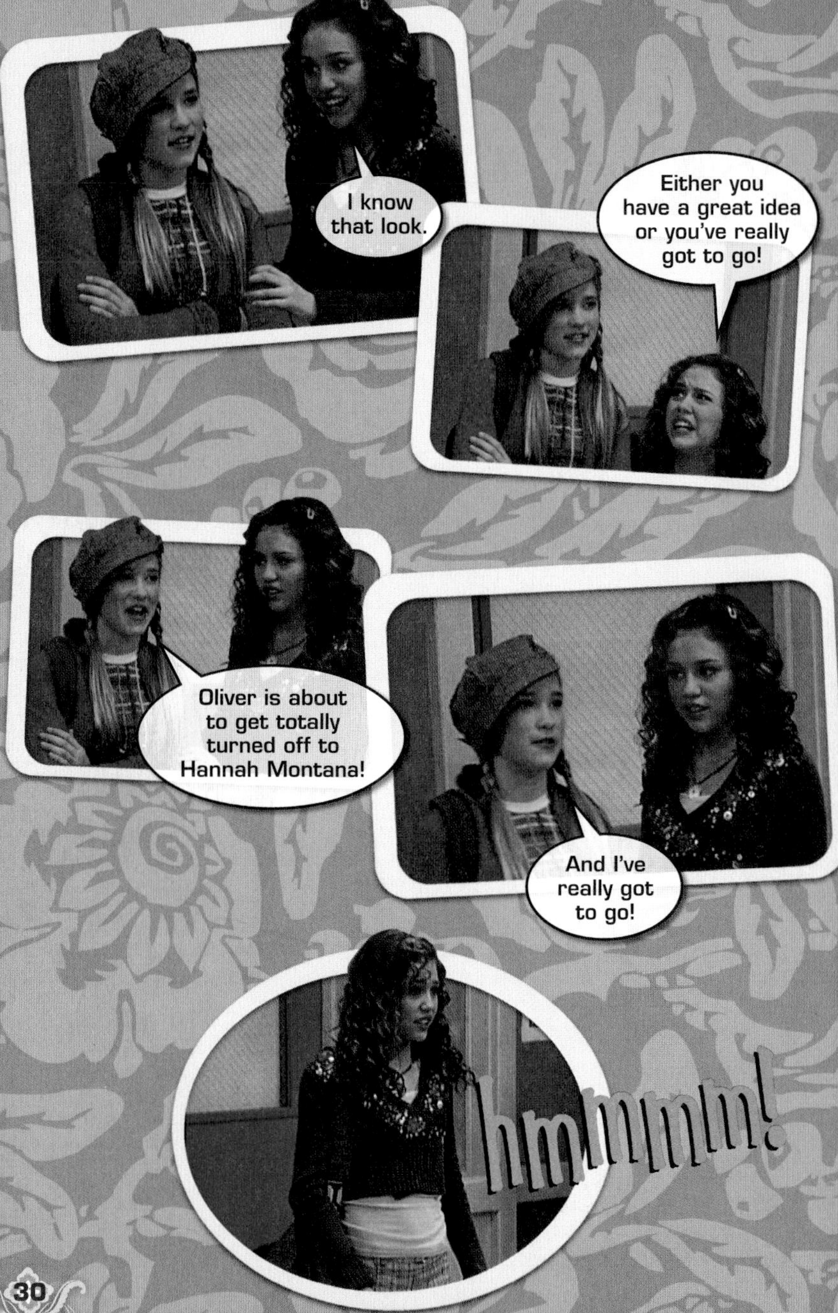
I know that look.
Either you have a great idea or you've really got to go!
Oliver is about to get totally turned off to Hannah Montana!
And I've really got to go!
hmmmm!

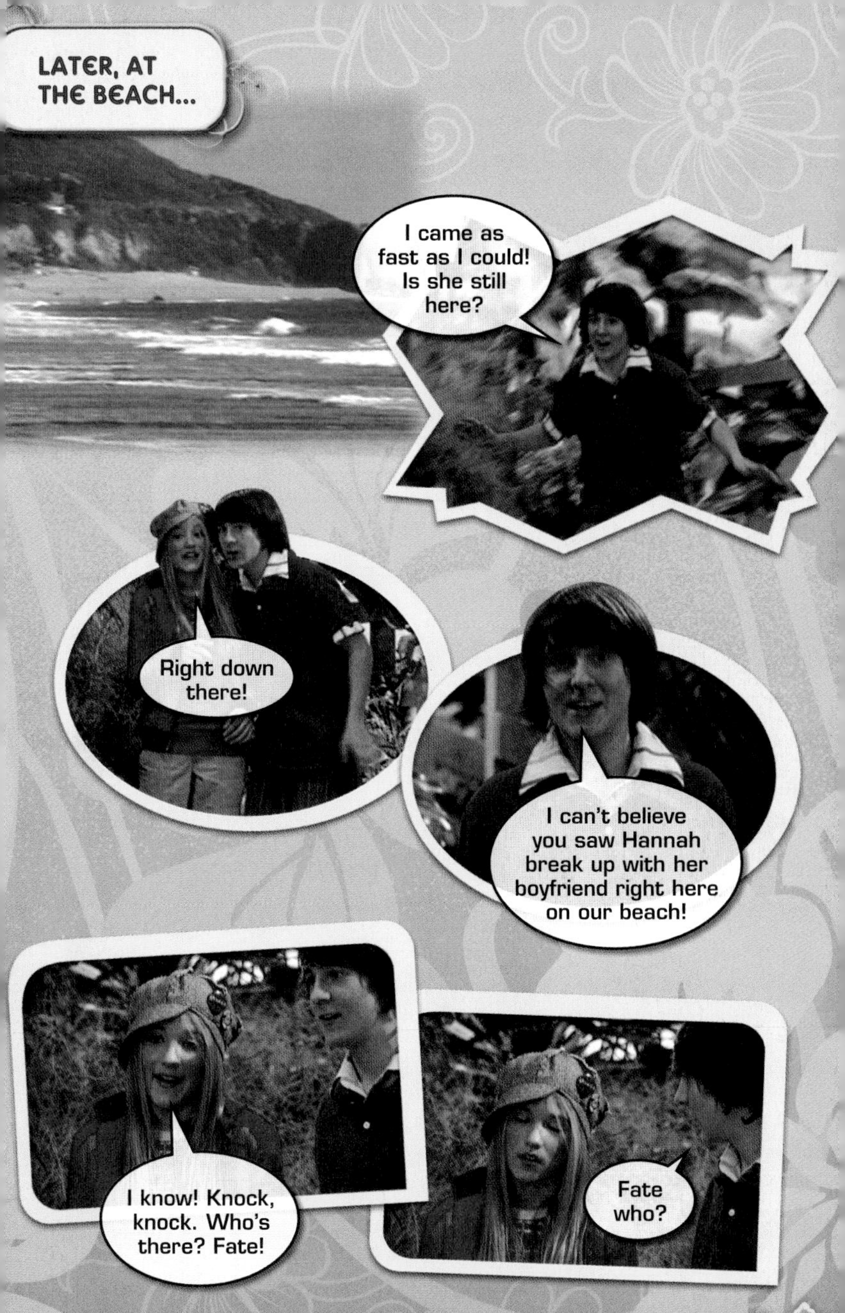
LATER, AT THE BEACH...
I came as fast as I could! Is she still here?
Right down there!
I can't believe you saw Hannah break up with her boyfriend right here on our beach!
I know! Knock, knock. Who's there? Fate!
Fate who?

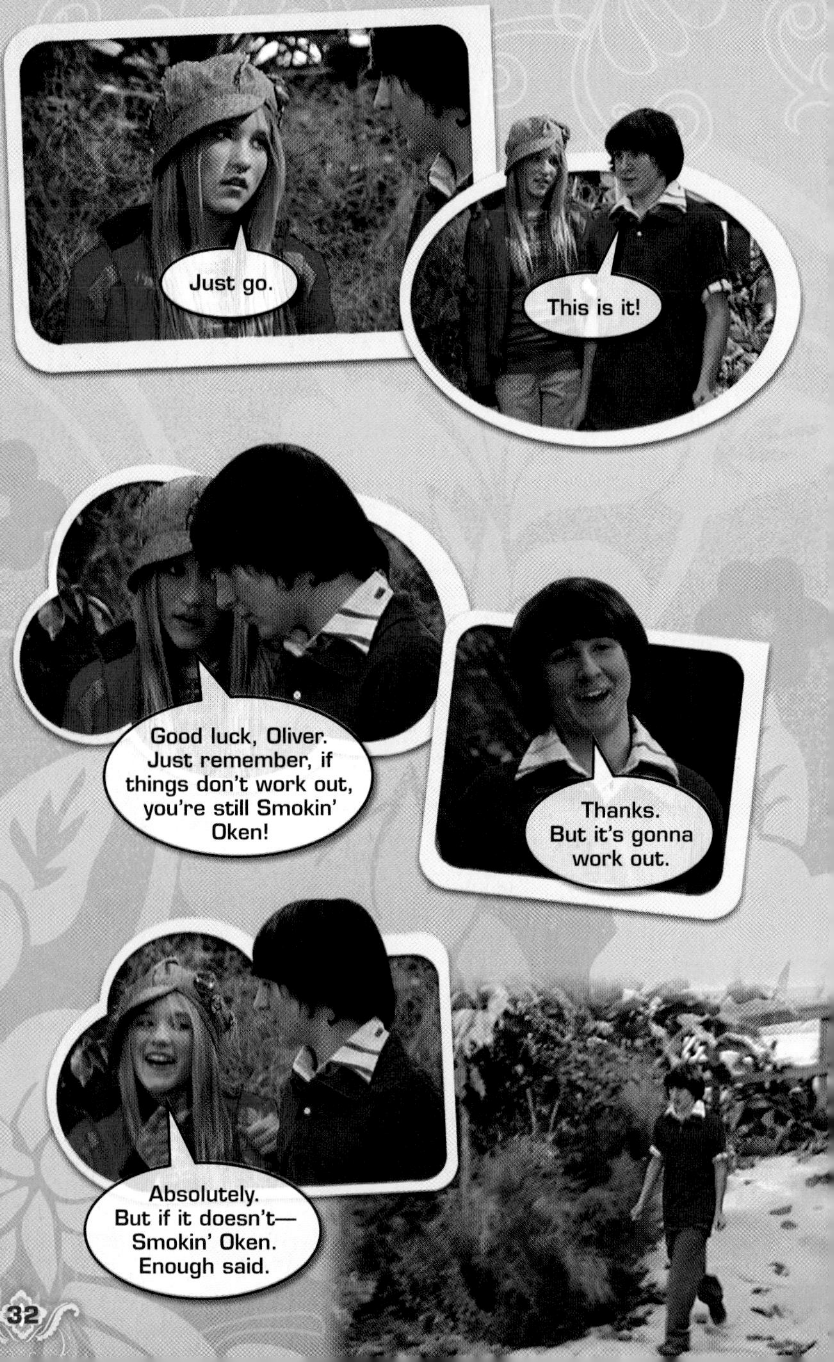
Just go.
This is it!
Good luck, Oliver. Just remember, if things don't work out, you're still Smokin' Oken!
Thanks. But it's gonna work out.
Absolutely. But if it doesn't— Smokin' Oken. Enough said.

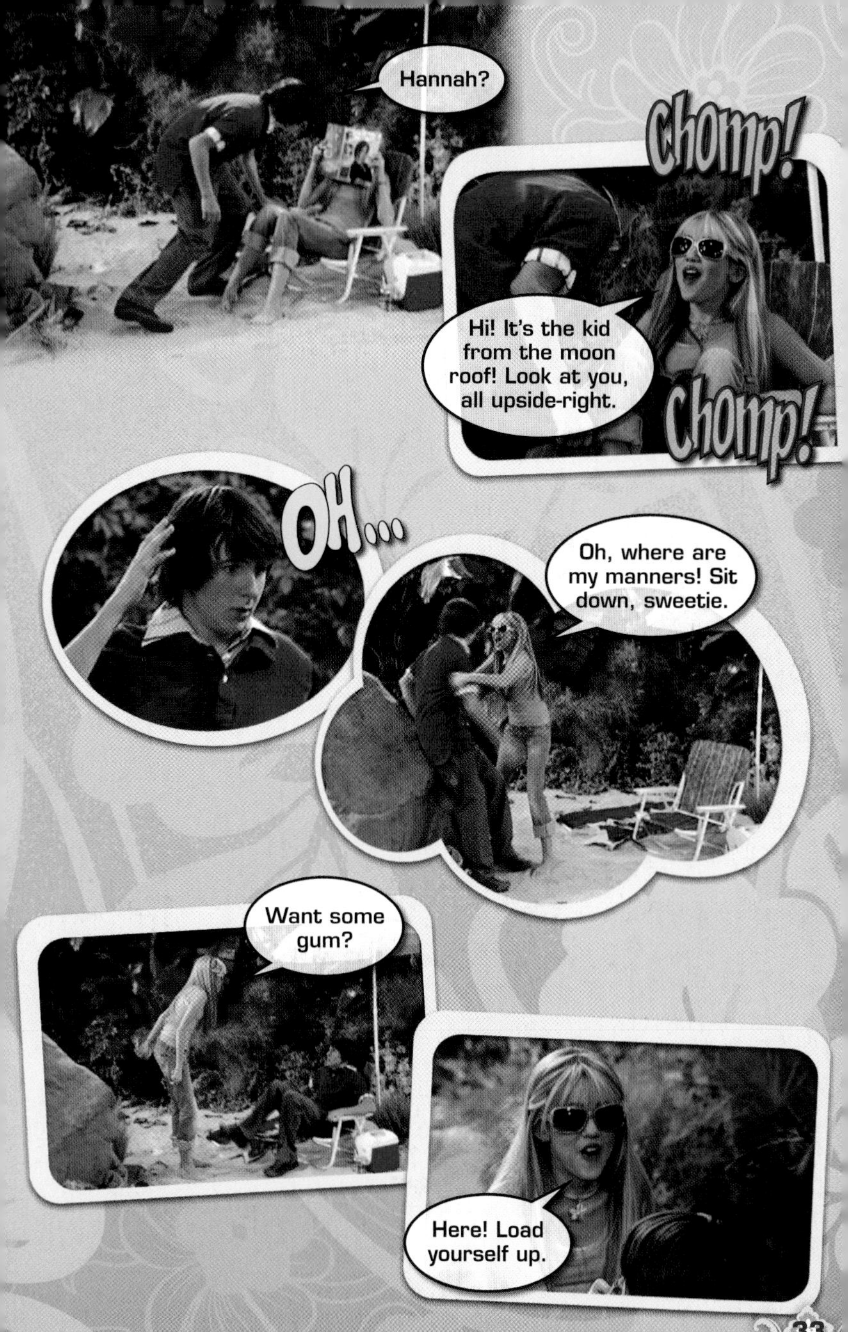
Hannah?
Chomp!
Hi! It's the kid from the moon roof! Look at you, all upside-right.
Chomp!
OH...
Oh, where are my manners! Sit down, sweetie.
Want some gum?
Here! Load yourself up.

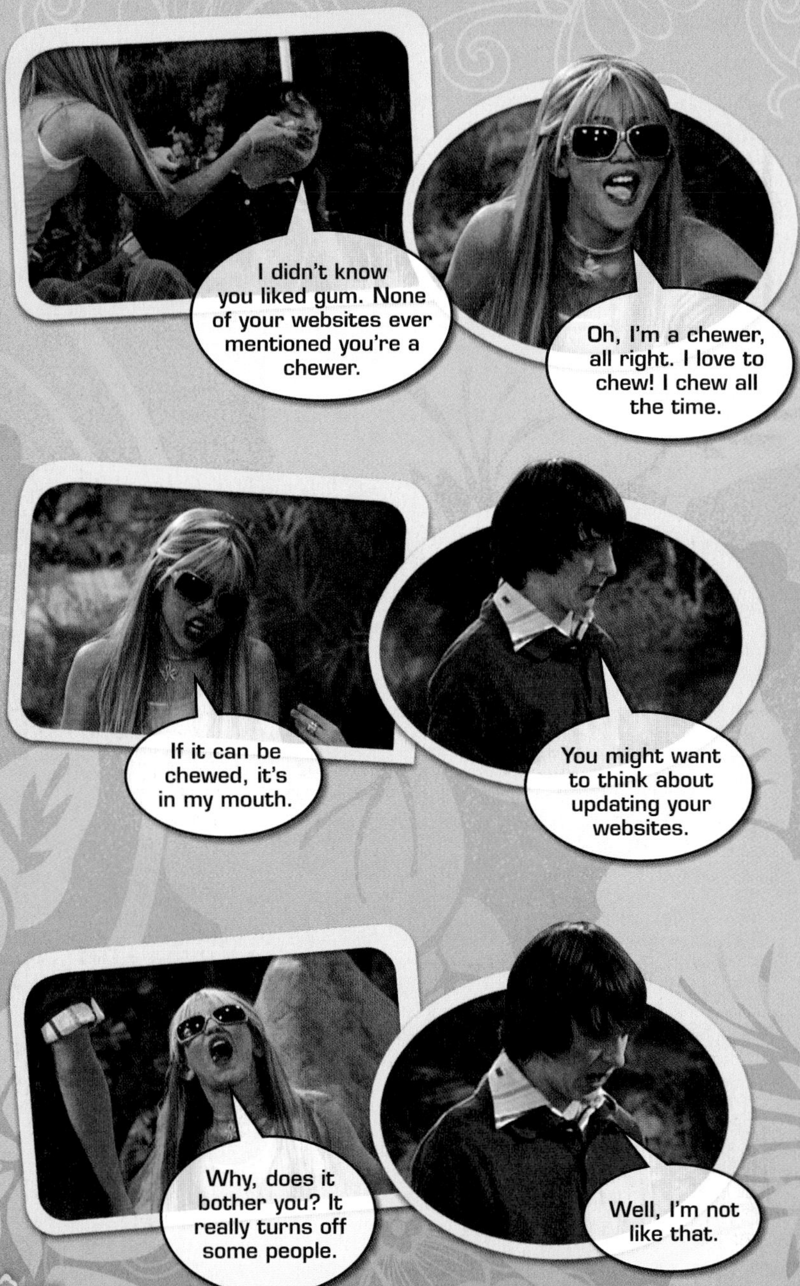
I didn't know you liked gum. None of your websites ever mentioned you're a chewer.
Oh, I'm a chewer, all right. I love to chew! I chew all the time.
If it can be chewed, it's in my mouth.
You might want to think about updating your websites.
Why, does it bother you? It really turns off some people.
Well, I'm not like that.

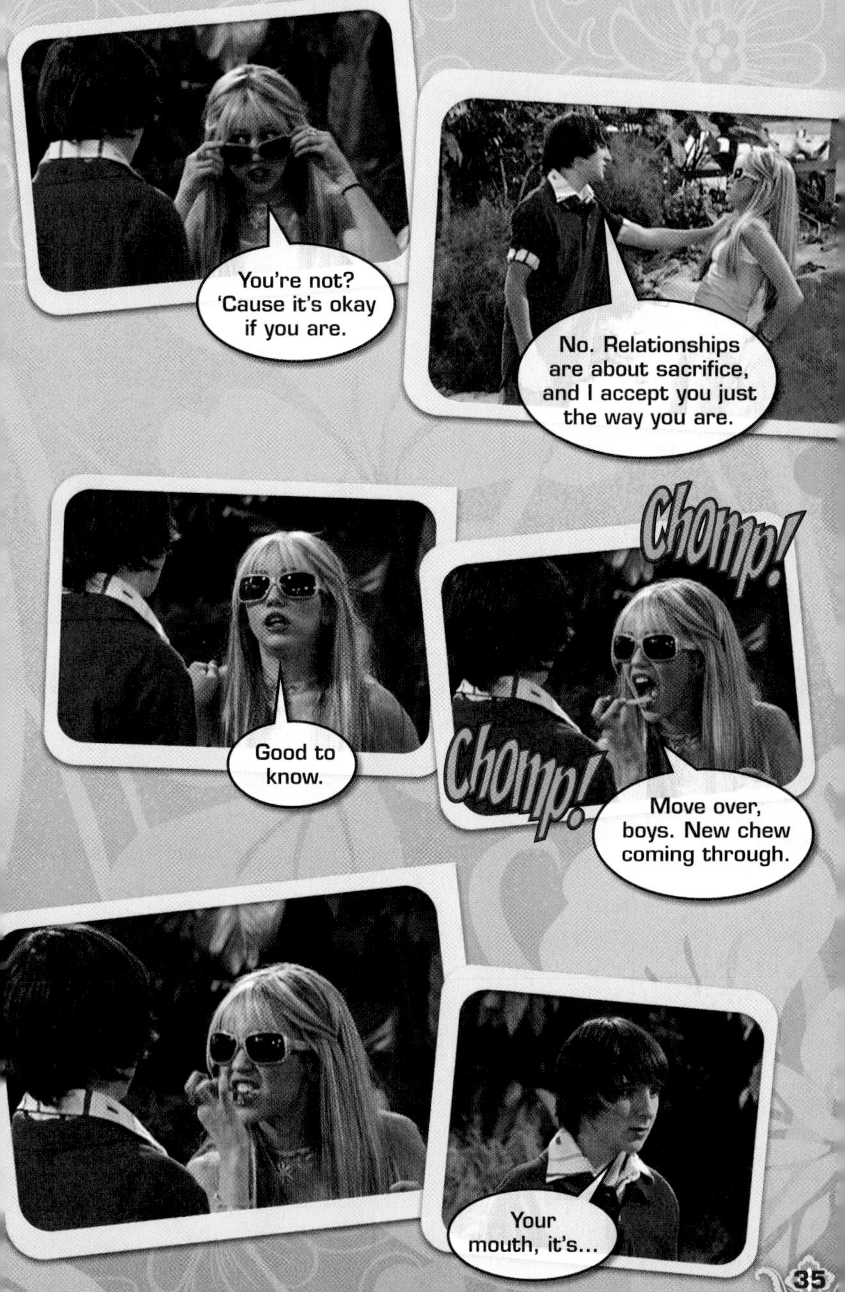
You're not? 'Cause it's okay if you are.
No. Relationships are about sacrifice, and I accept you just the way you are.
Good to know.
Chomp!
Chomp!
Move over, boys. New chew coming through.
Your mouth, it's...

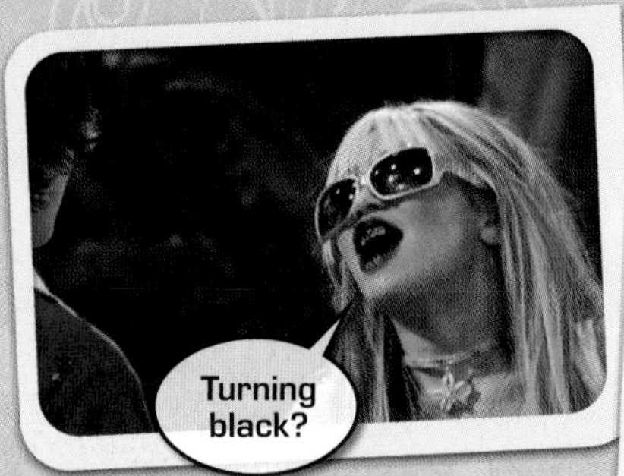
Turning black?

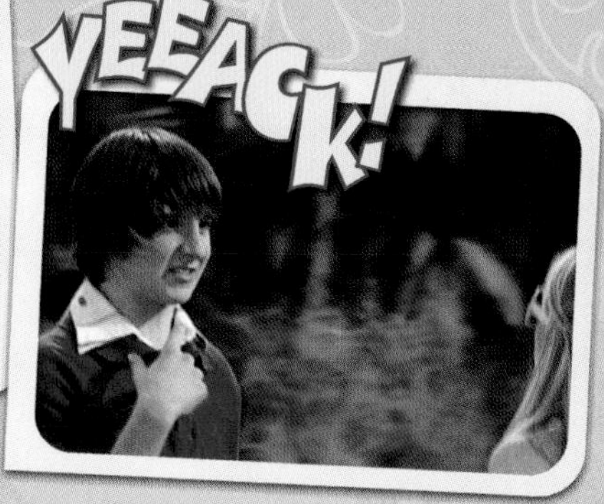
YEEACK!

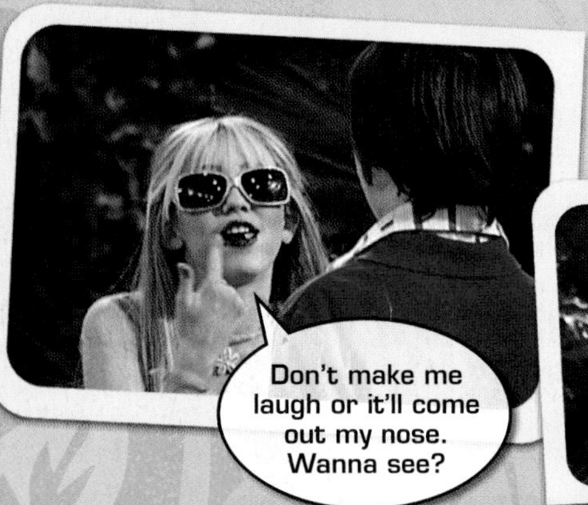
Don't make me laugh or it'll come out my nose. Wanna see?

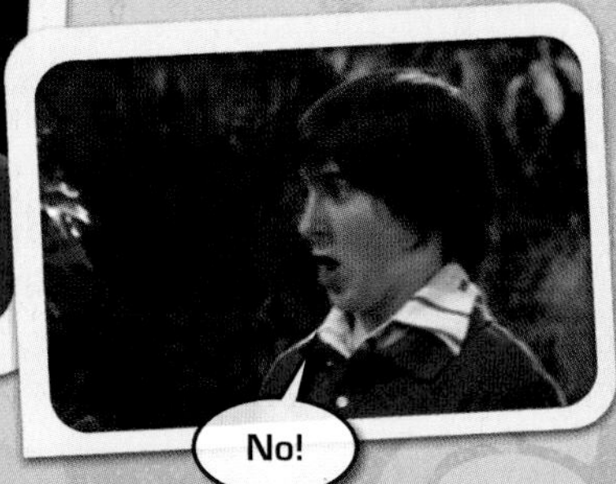
No!

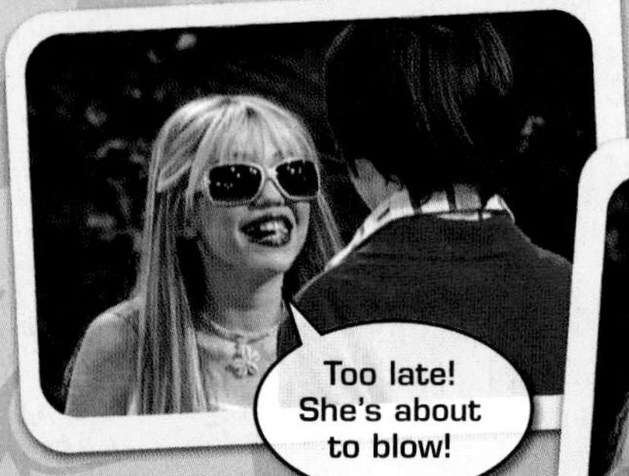
Too late! She's about to blow!

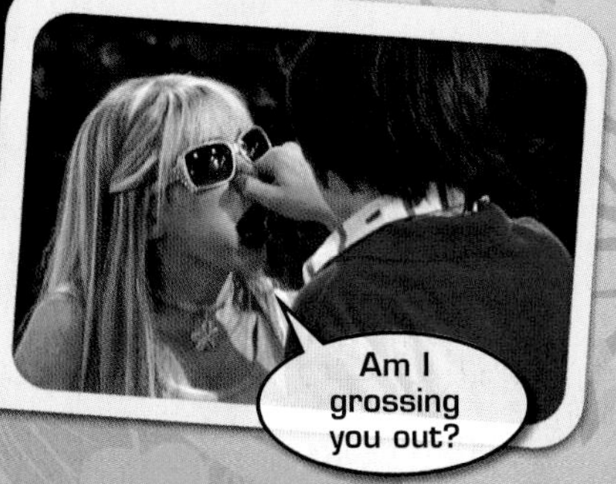
Am I grossing you out?

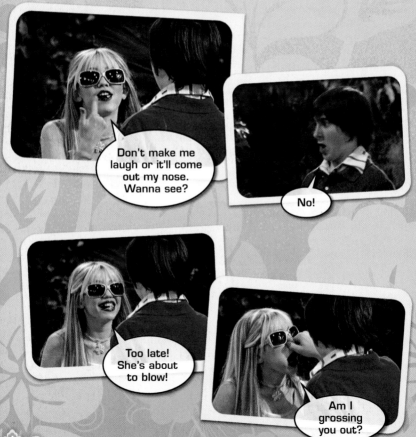

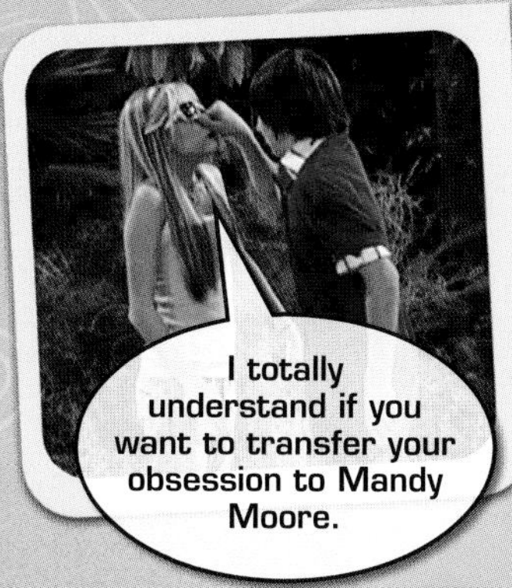
I totally understand if you want to transfer your obsession to Mandy Moore.

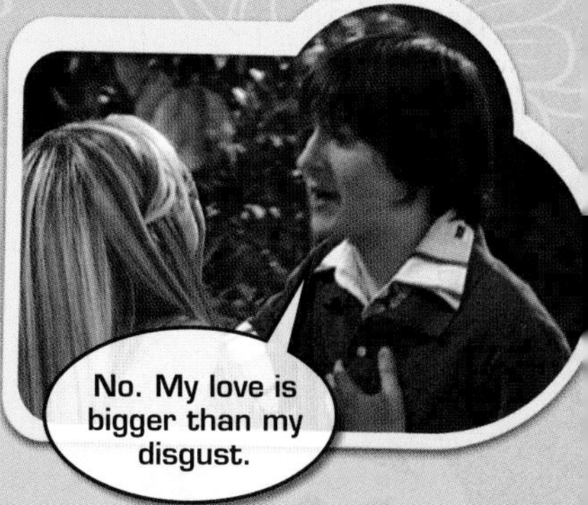
No. My love is bigger than my disgust.

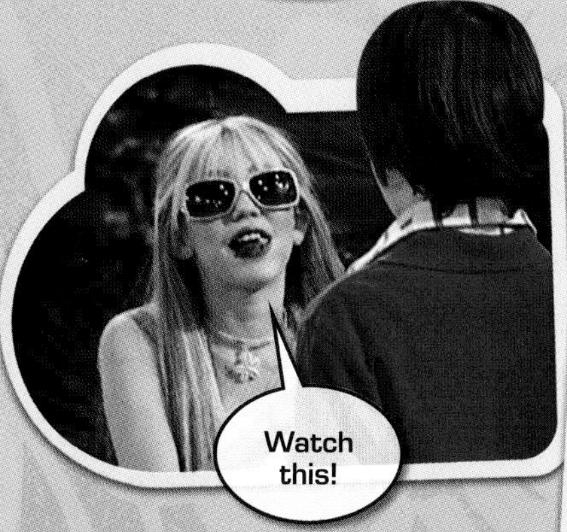
Watch this!

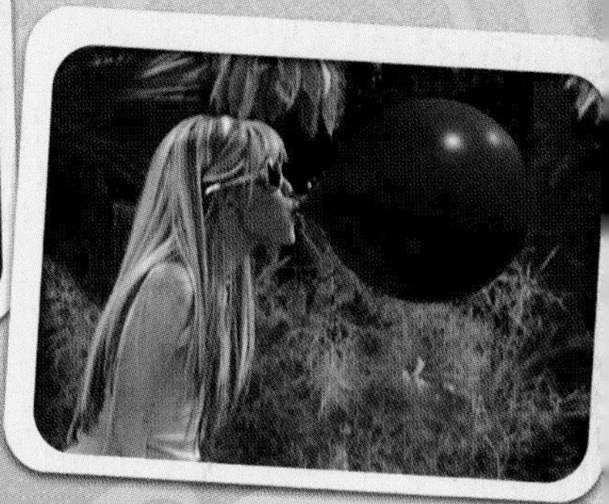

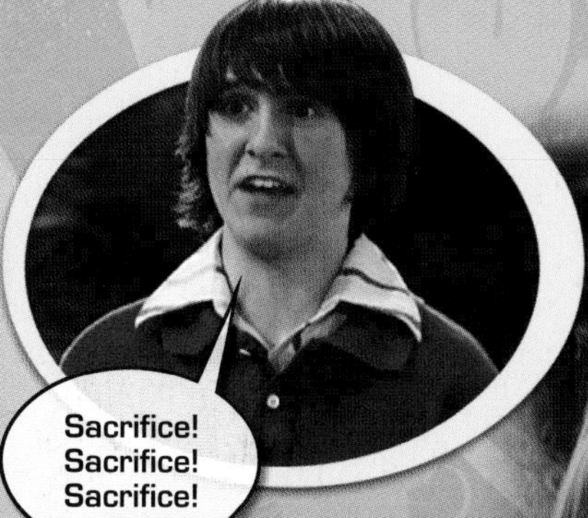
Sacrifice!
Sacrifice!
Sacrifice!

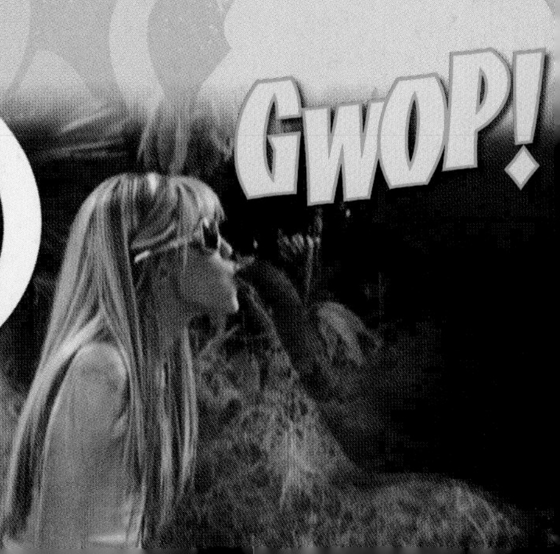
GWOP!

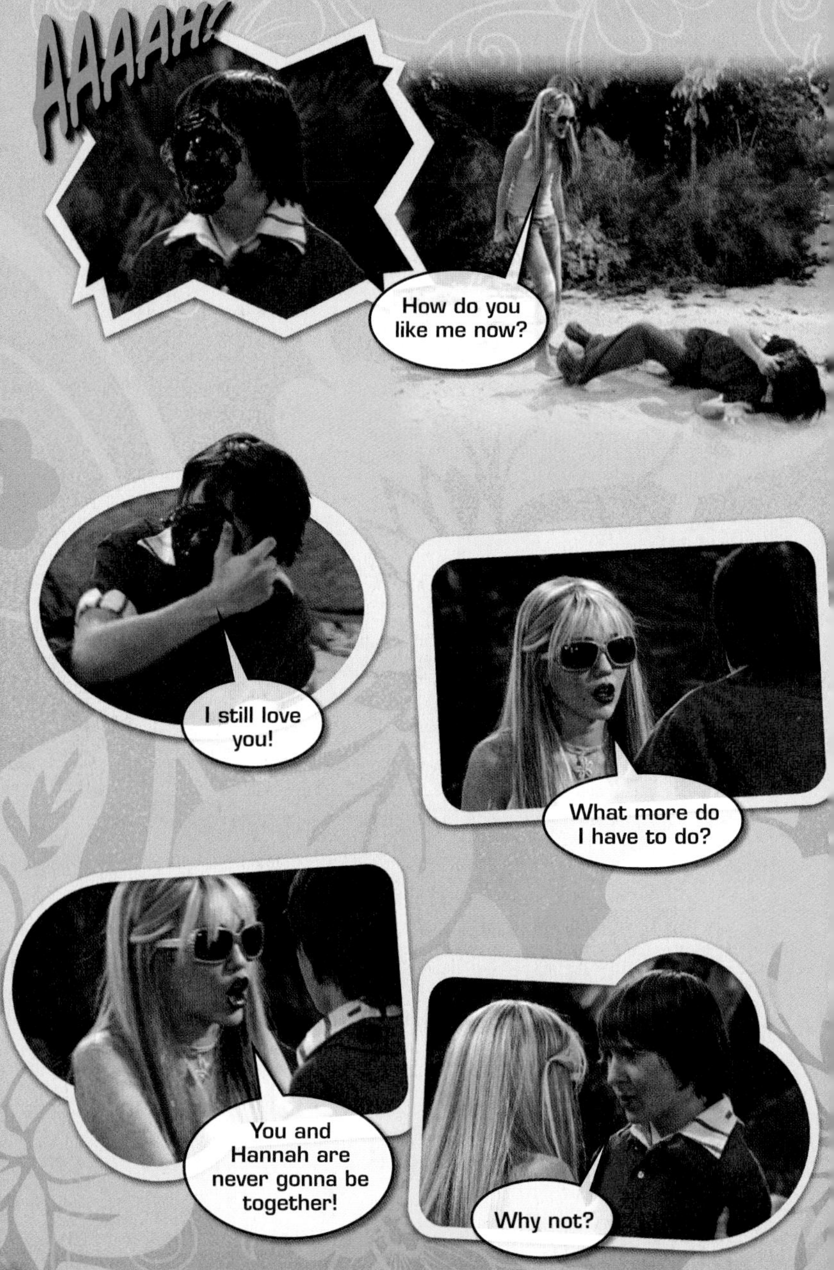
AAAAH!
How do you like me now?
I still love you!
What more do I have to do?
You and Hannah are never gonna be together!
Why not?

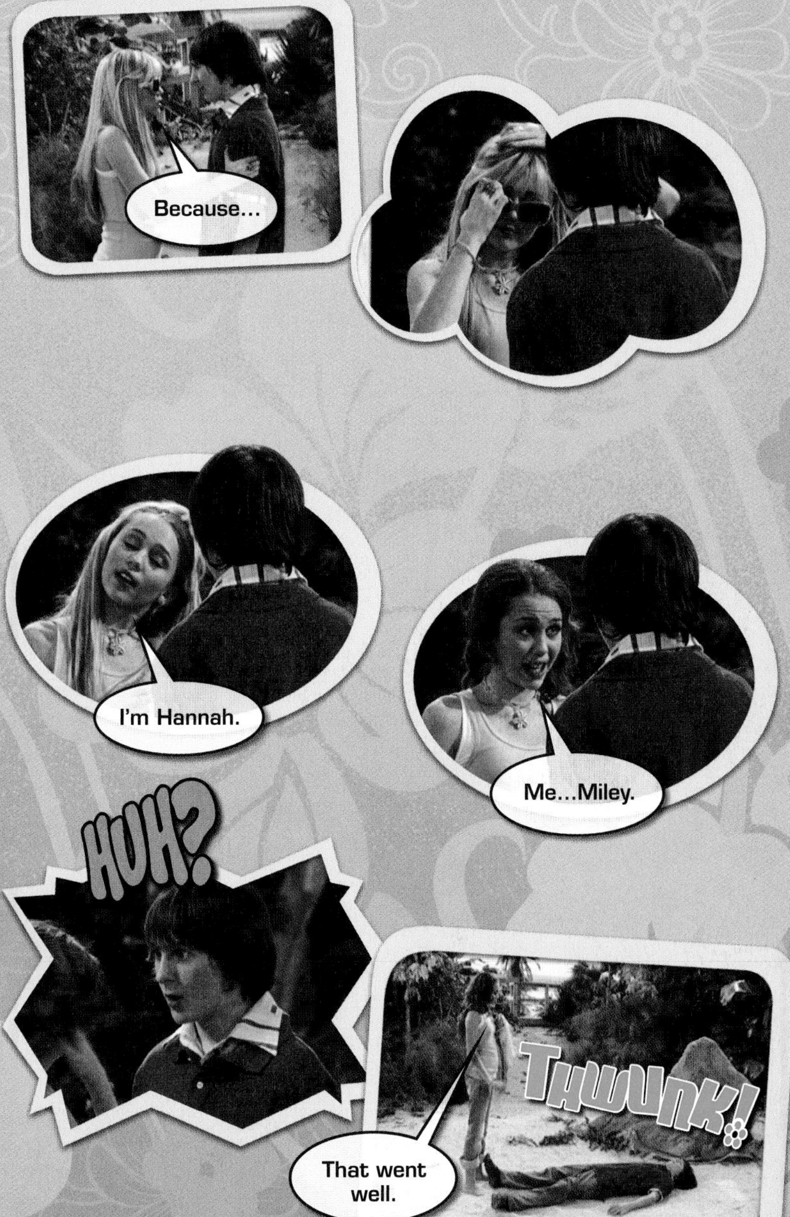
Because...
I'm Hannah.
Me...Miley.
HUH?
That went well.
THWUNK!

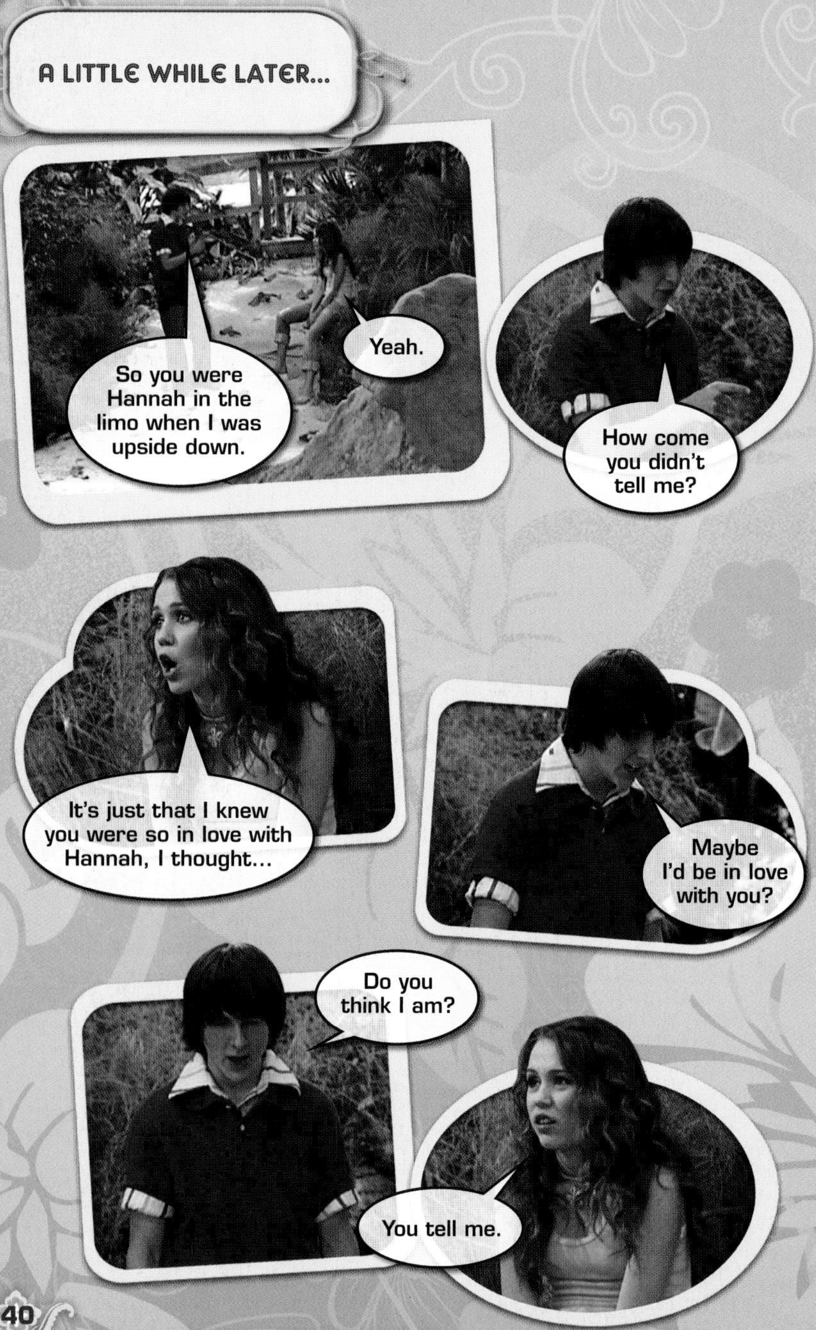
A LITTLE WHILE LATER...
So you were Hannah in the limo when I was upside down.
Yeah.
How come you didn't tell me?
It's just that I knew you were so in love with Hannah, I thought...
Maybe I'd be in love with you?
Do you think I am?
You tell me.

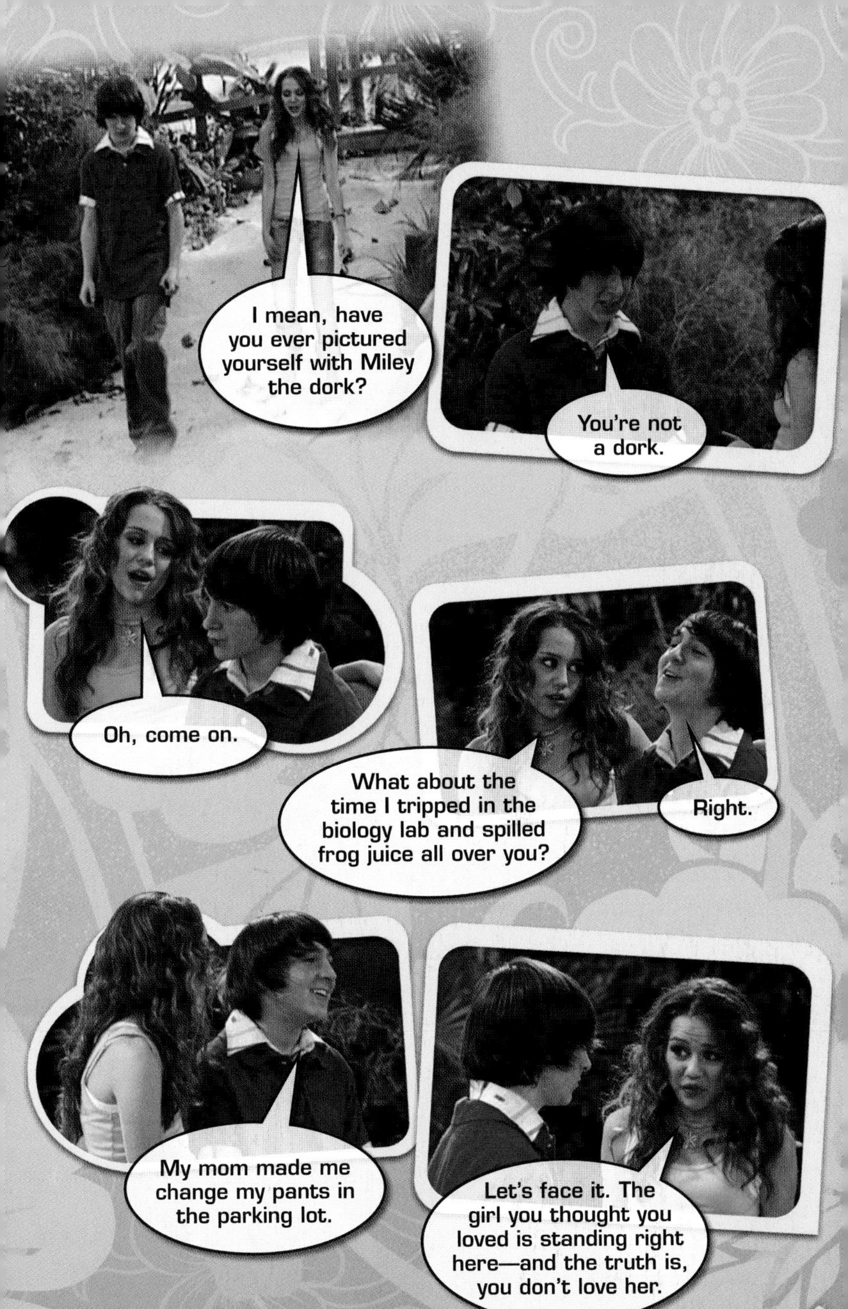
I mean, have you ever pictured yourself with Miley the dork?
You're not a dork.
Oh, come on.
What about the time I tripped in the biology lab and spilled frog juice all over you?
Right.
My mom made me change my pants in the parking lot.
Let's face it. The girl you thought you loved is standing right here—and the truth is, you don't love her.

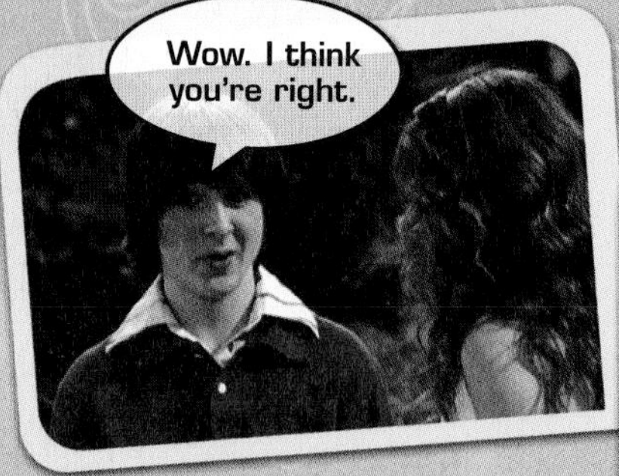
Wow. I think you're right.

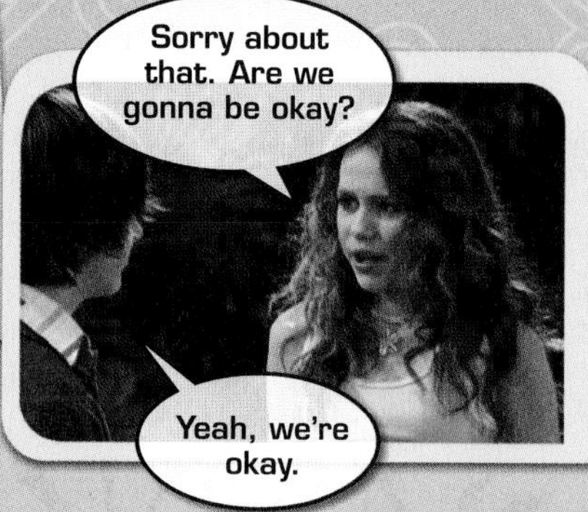
Sorry about that. Are we gonna be okay?
Yeah, we're okay.

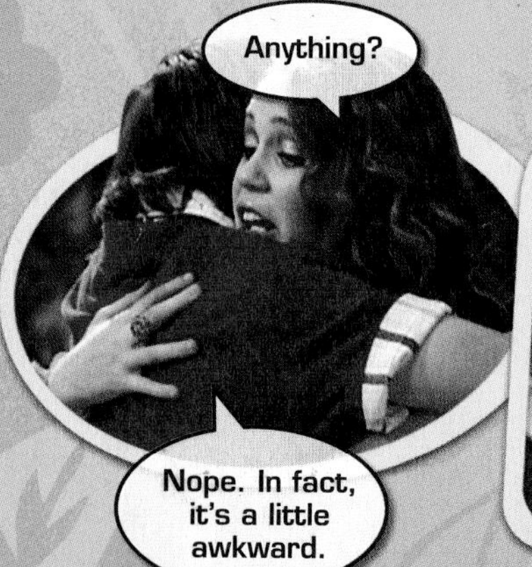
Anything?
Nope. In fact, it's a little awkward.

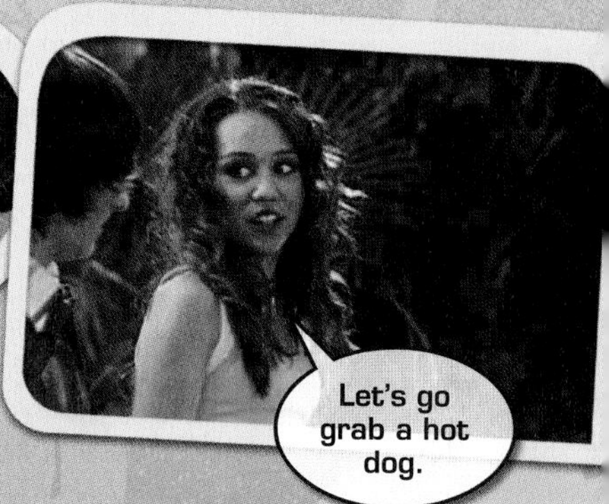
Let's go grab a hot dog.

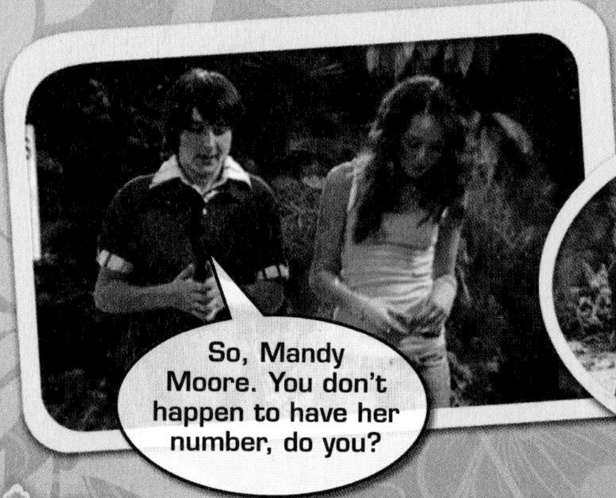
So, Mandy Moore. You don't happen to have her number, do you?

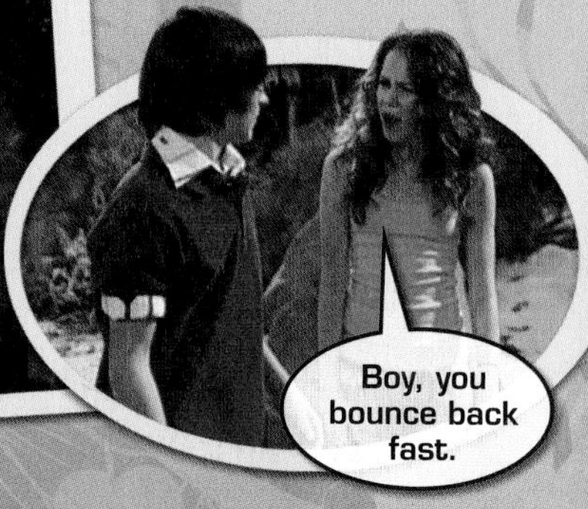
Boy, you bounce back fast.

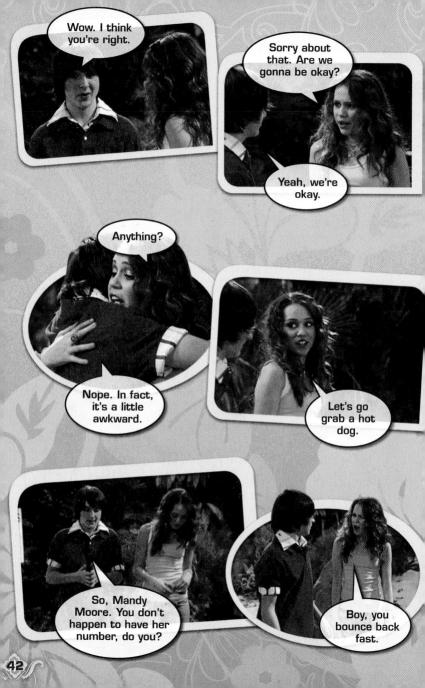

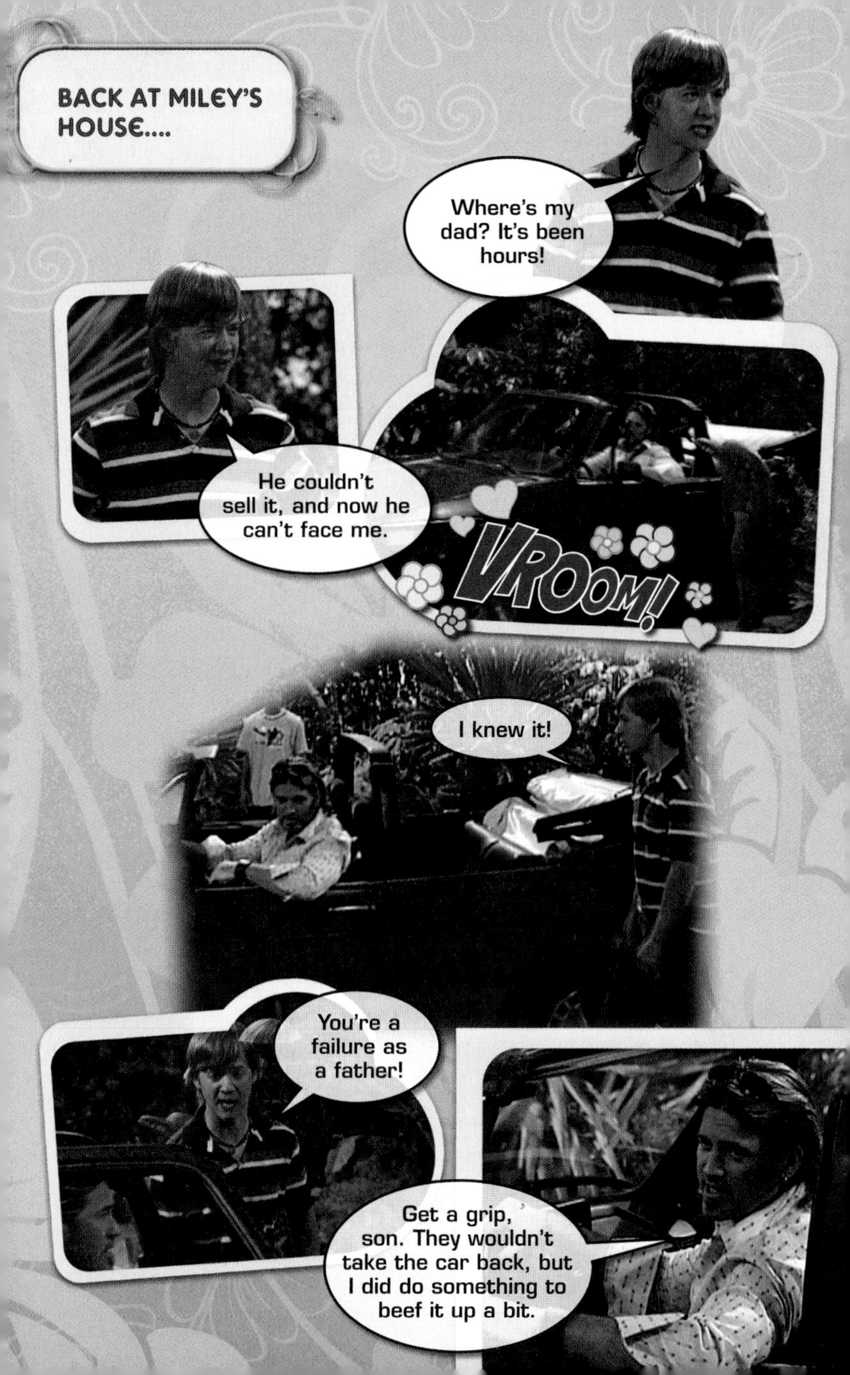
BACK AT MILEY'S HOUSE....
Where's my dad? It's been hours!
He couldn't sell it, and now he can't face me.
VROOM!
I knew it!
You're a failure as a father!
Get a grip, son. They wouldn't take the car back, but I did do something to beef it up a bit.

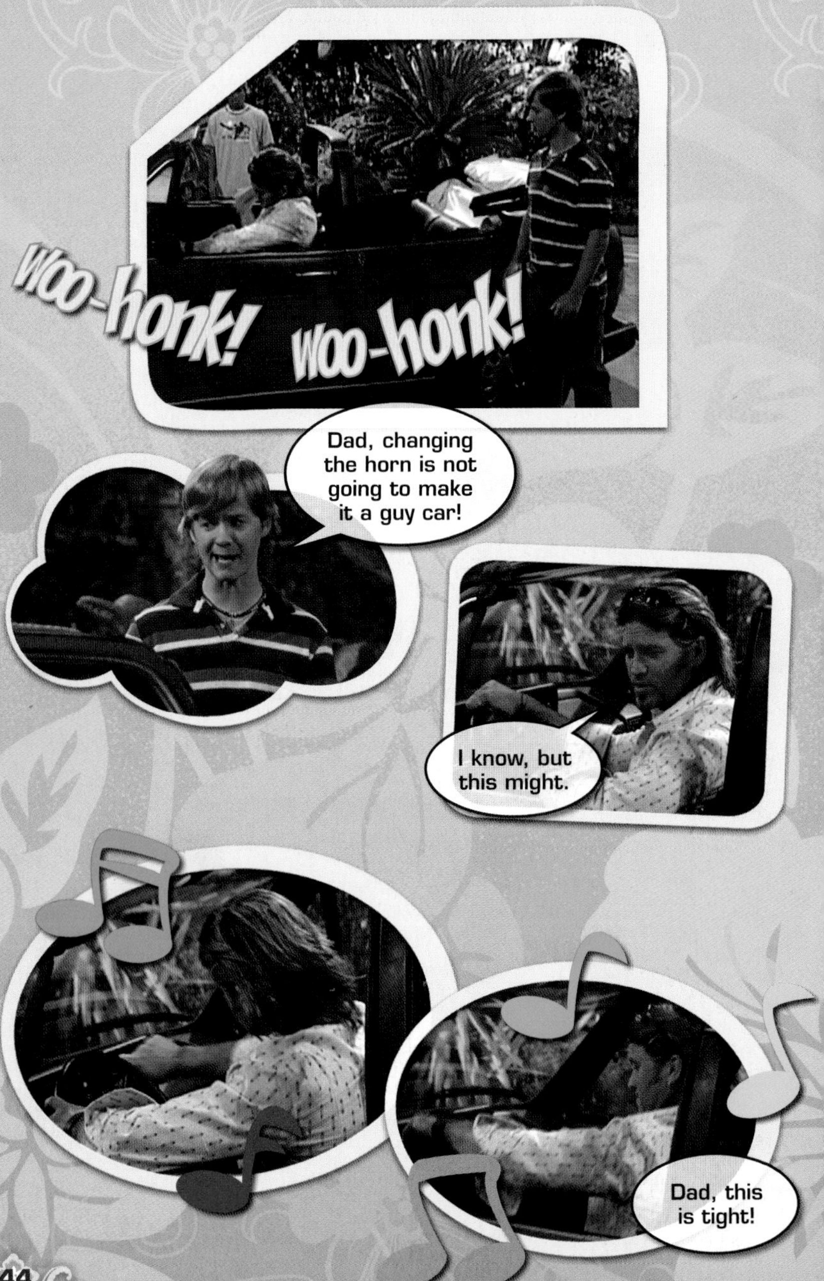
Woo-honk! Woo-honk!
Dad, changing the horn is not going to make it a guy car!
I know, but this might.
Dad, this is tight!

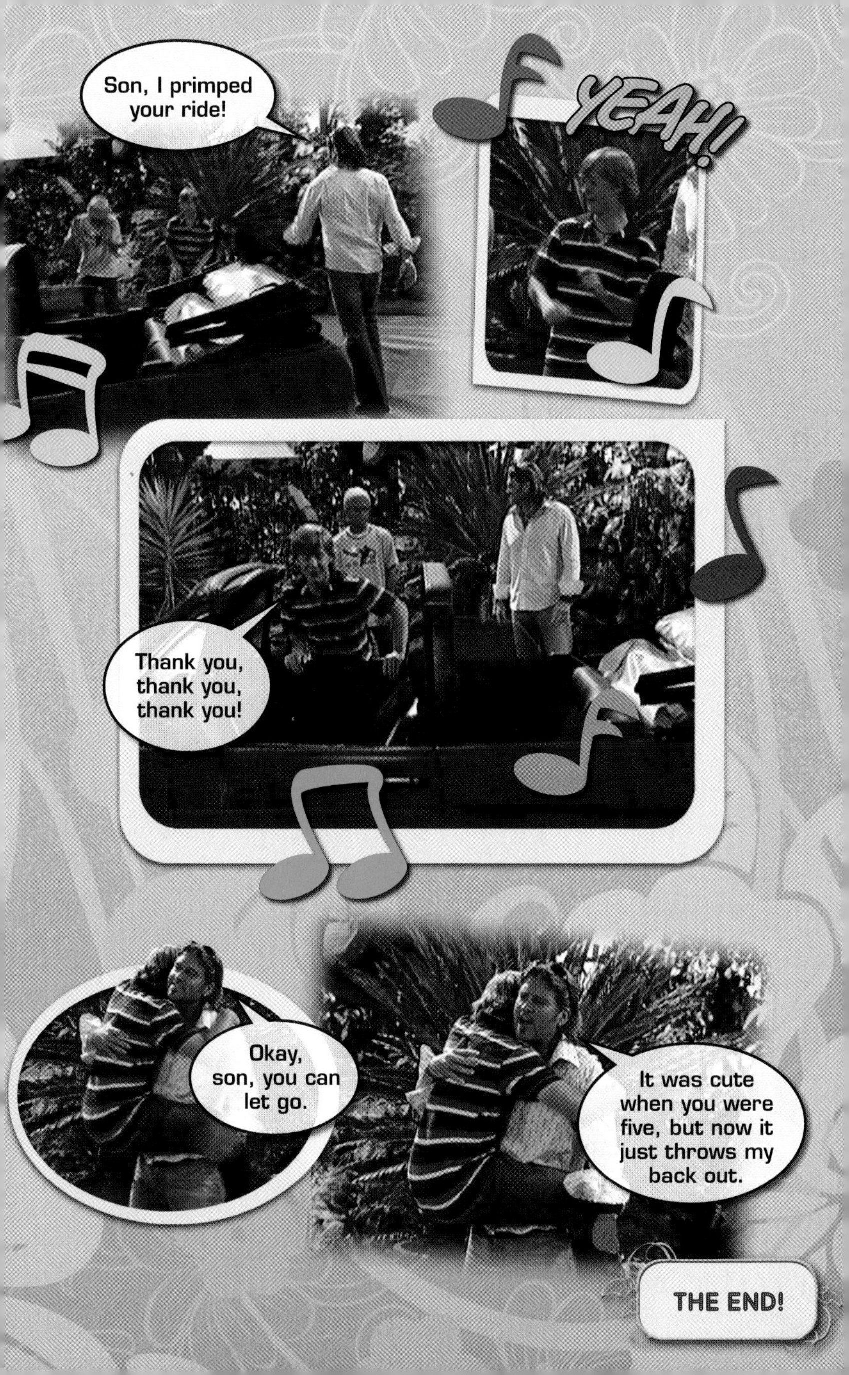
Son, I primped your ride!
YEAH!
Thank you, thank you, thank you!
Okay, son, you can let go.
It was cute when you were five, but now it just throws my back out.
THE END!

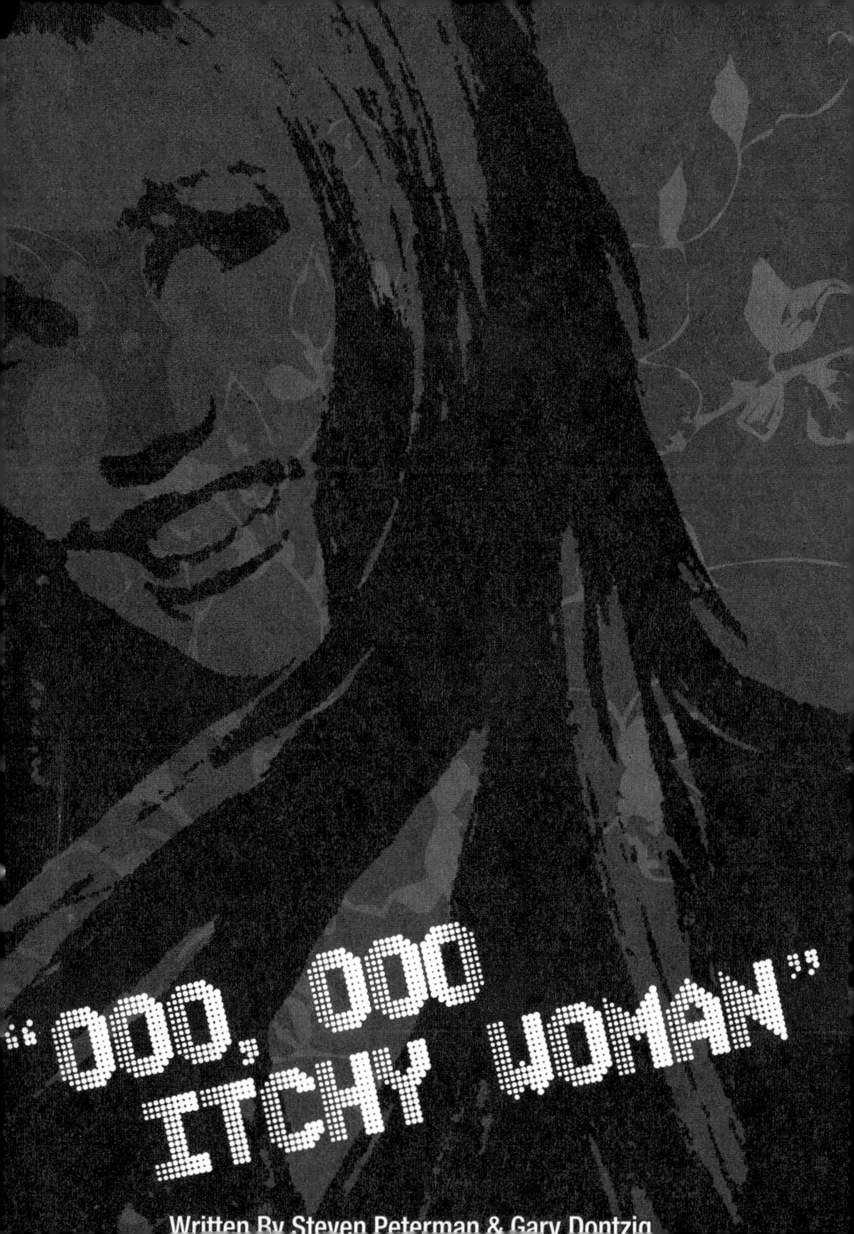

"OOO, OOO ITCHY WOMAN"

Written By Steven Peterman & Gary Dontzig

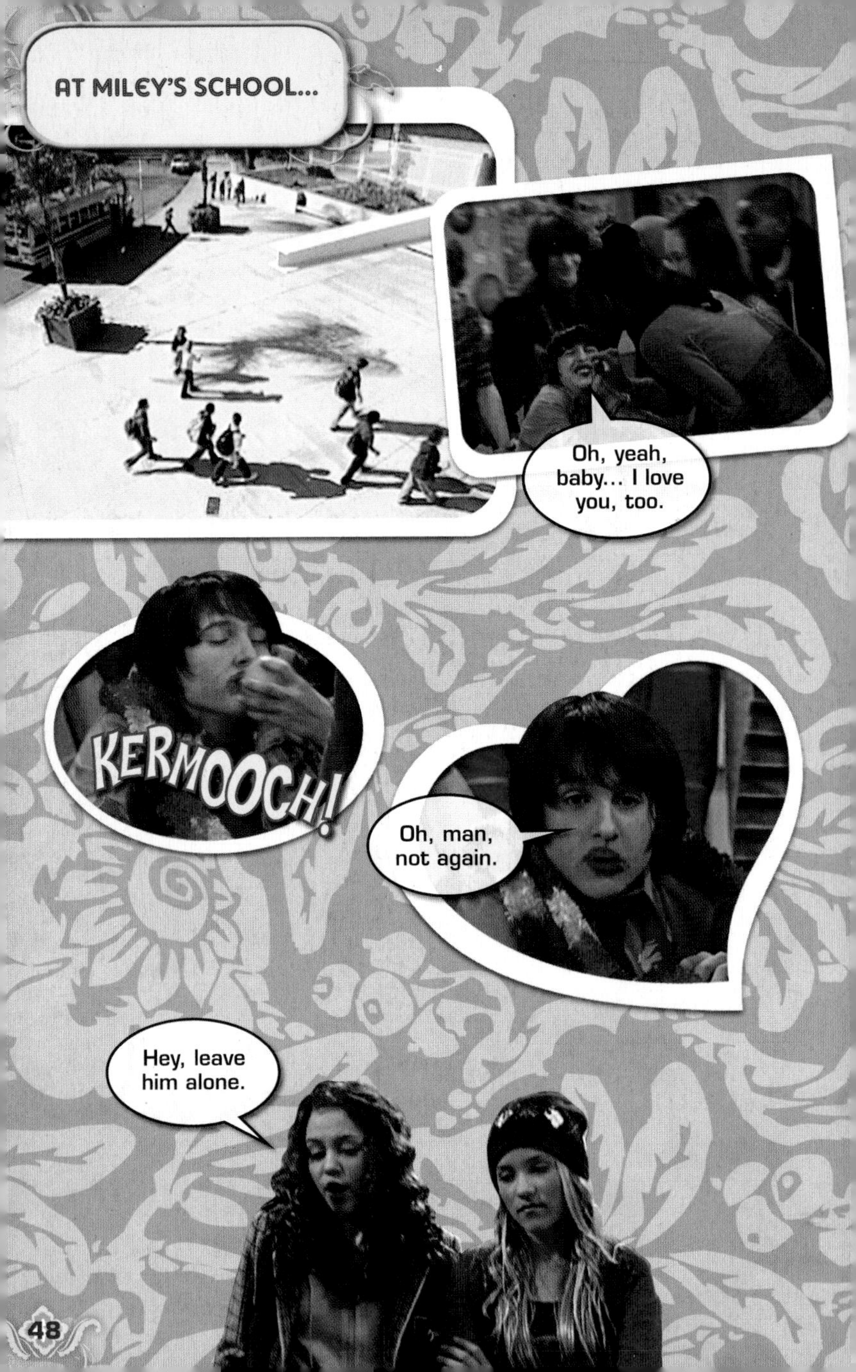
AT MILEY'S SCHOOL...
Oh, yeah, baby... I love you, too.
KERMOOCH!
Oh, man, not again.
Hey, leave him alone.

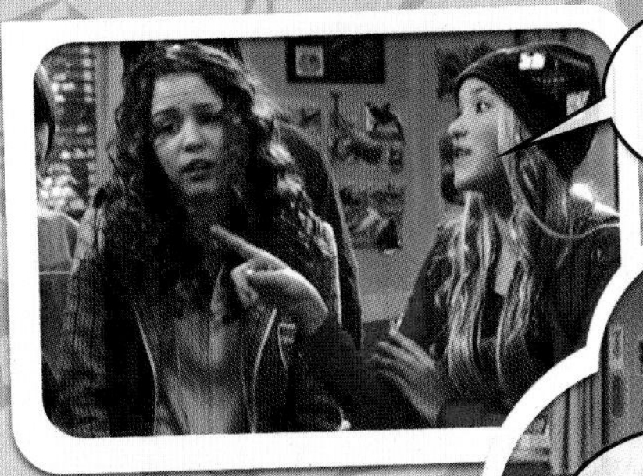
Yeah, nobody picks on Oliver but us.

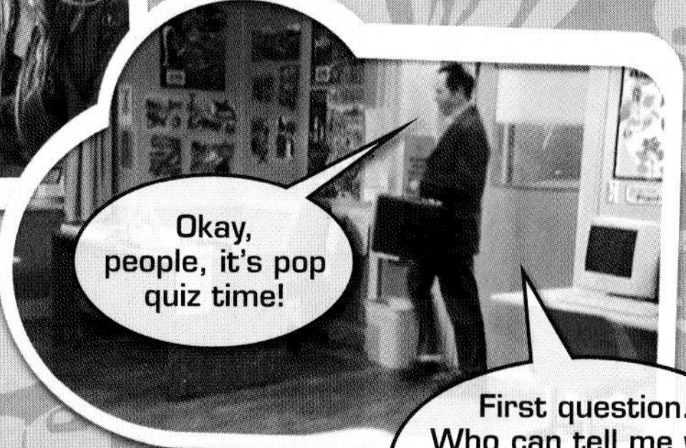
Okay, people, it's pop quiz time!
First question. Who can tell me wh this is the worst day of my life?

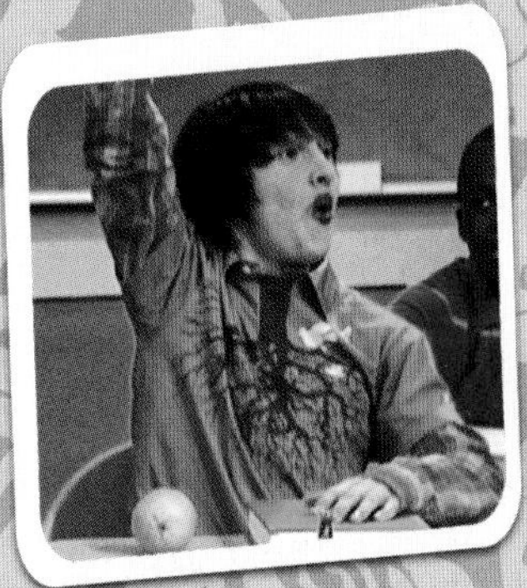

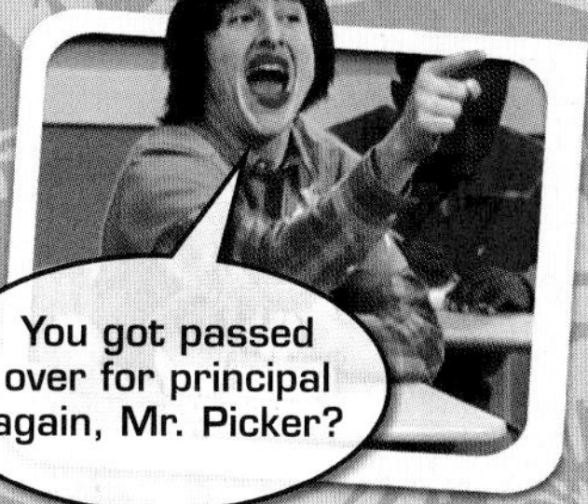
You got passed over for principal again, Mr. Picker?

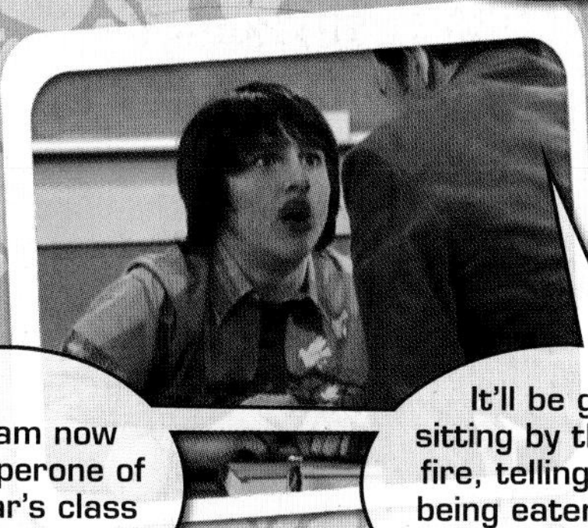
No, I am now the chaperone of this year's class camping trip.
It'll be great, sitting by the camp-fire, telling stories, being eaten alive by disease-ridden bugs.

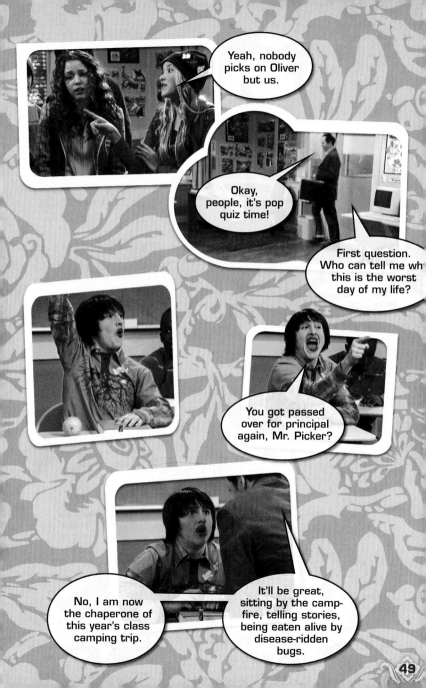

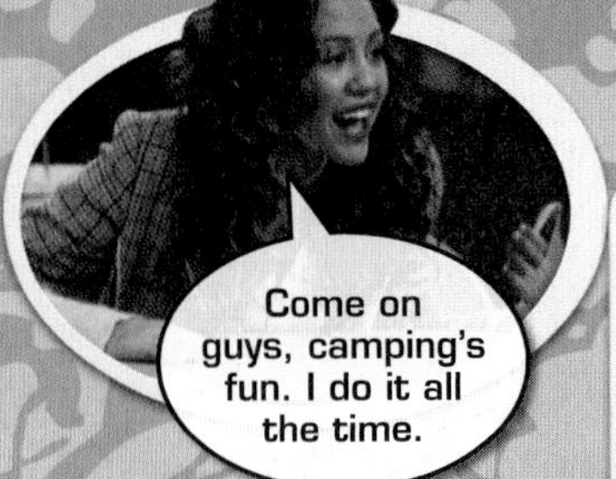
Come on guys, camping's fun. I do it all the time.

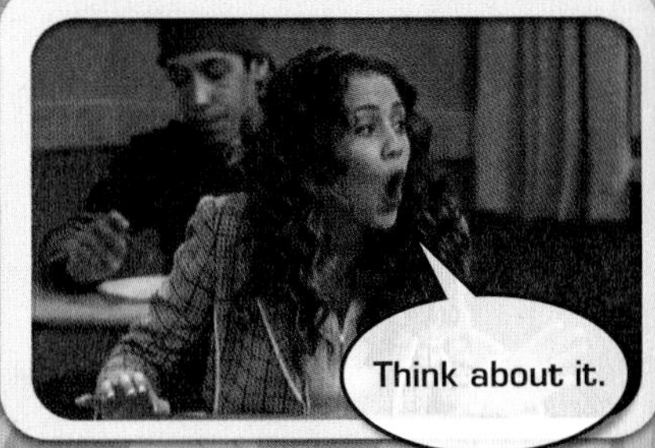
Think about it.

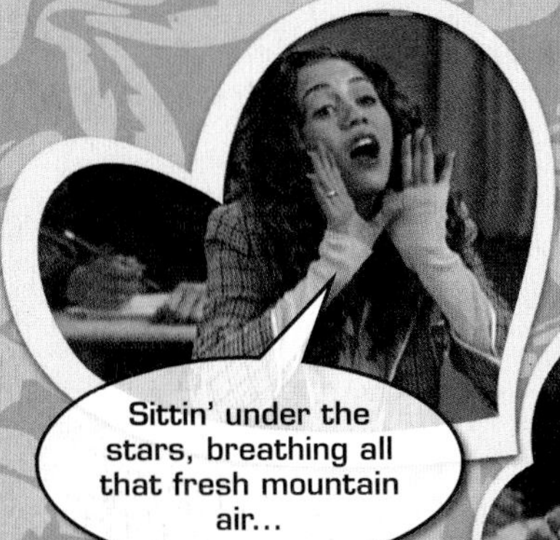
Sittin' under the stars, breathing all that fresh mountain air...

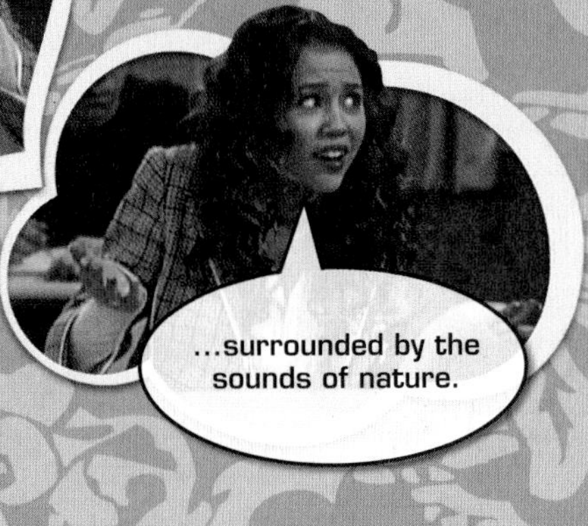
...surrounded by the sounds of nature.

AMBER AND ASHLEY CALL MILEY A HILLBILLY. WHEN LILLY DEFENDS HER, THEY ALL GET SCOLDED BY THEIR TEACHER, MR. PICKER. THEY TRY TO SWEET-TALK HIM.

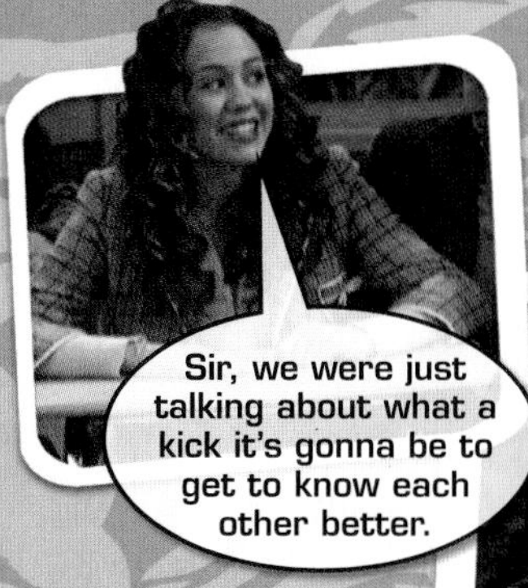
Sir, we were just talking about what a kick it's gonna be to get to know each other better.

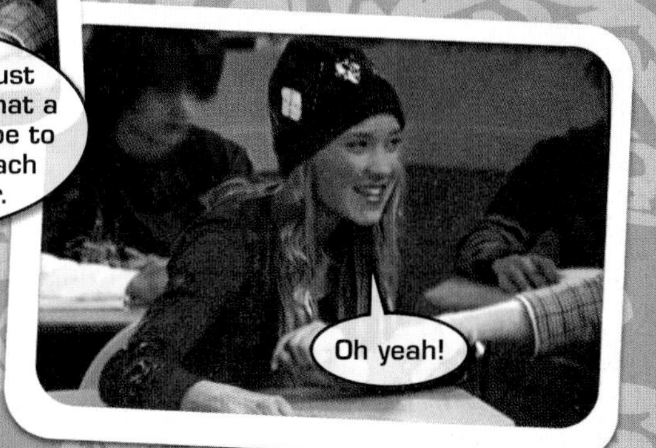
Oh yeah!

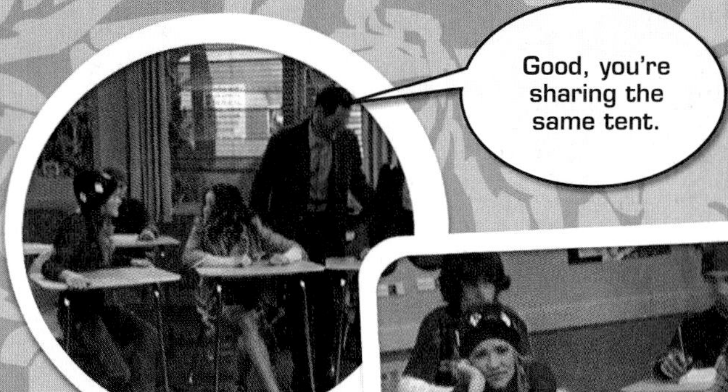
Good, you're sharing the same tent.

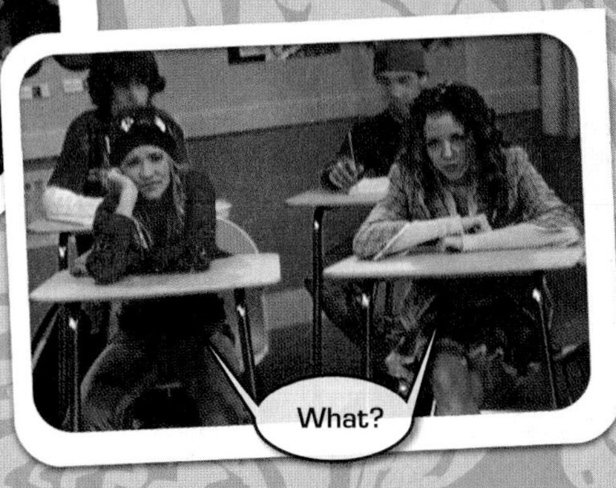
What?

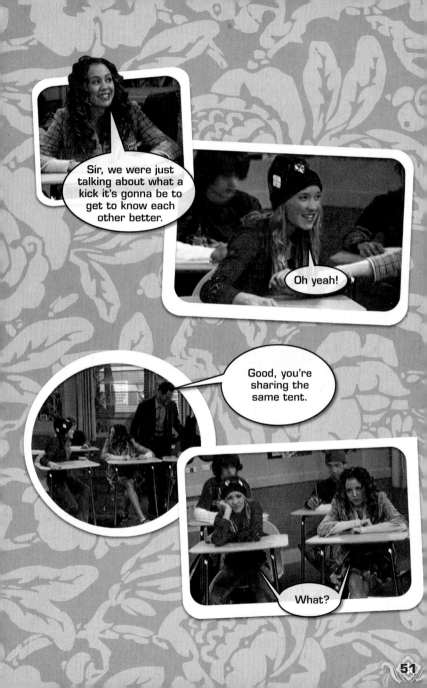

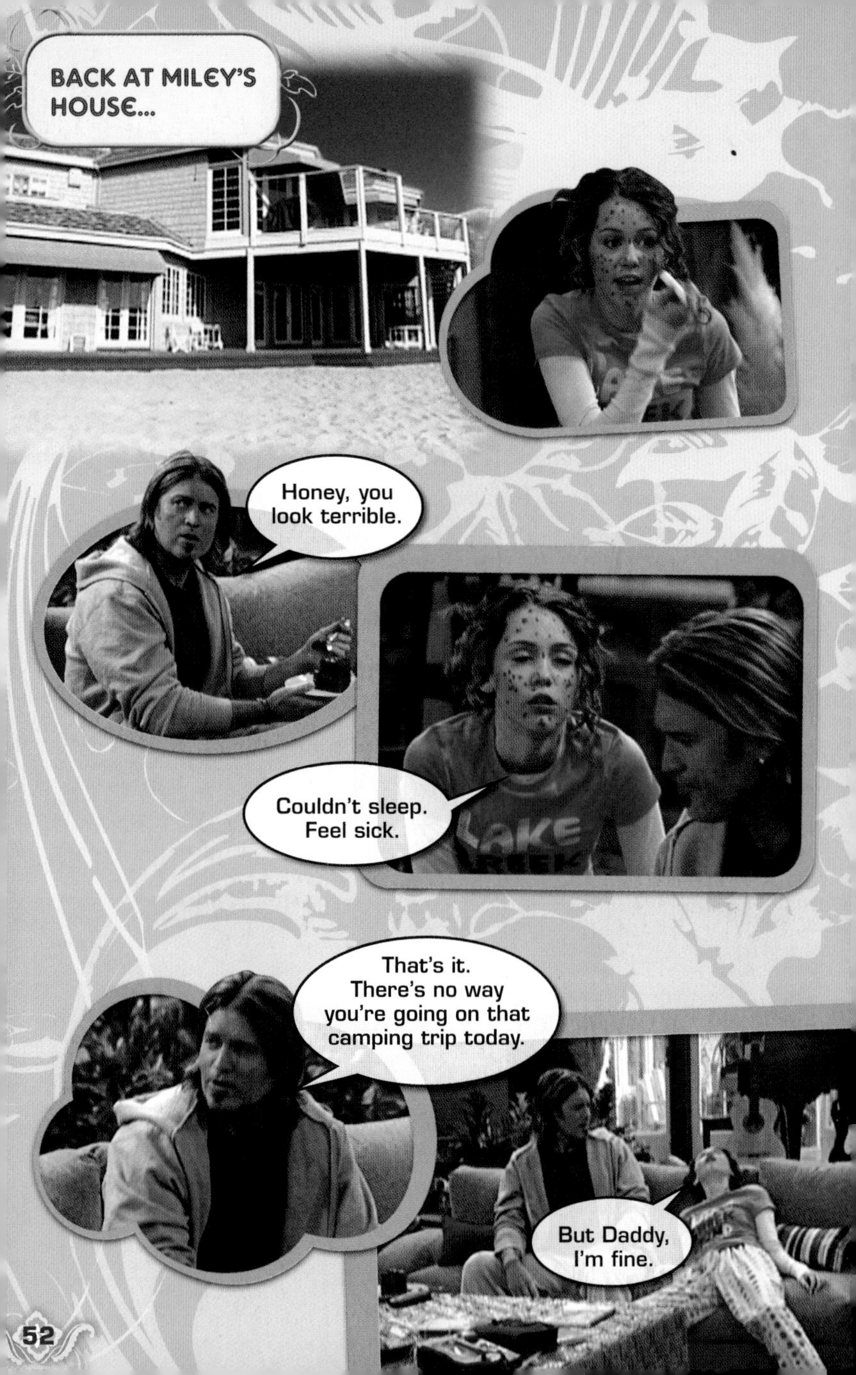
BACK AT MILEY'S HOUSE...
Honey, you look terrible.
Couldn't sleep. Feel sick.
That's it. There's no way you're going on that camping trip today.
But Daddy, I'm fine.

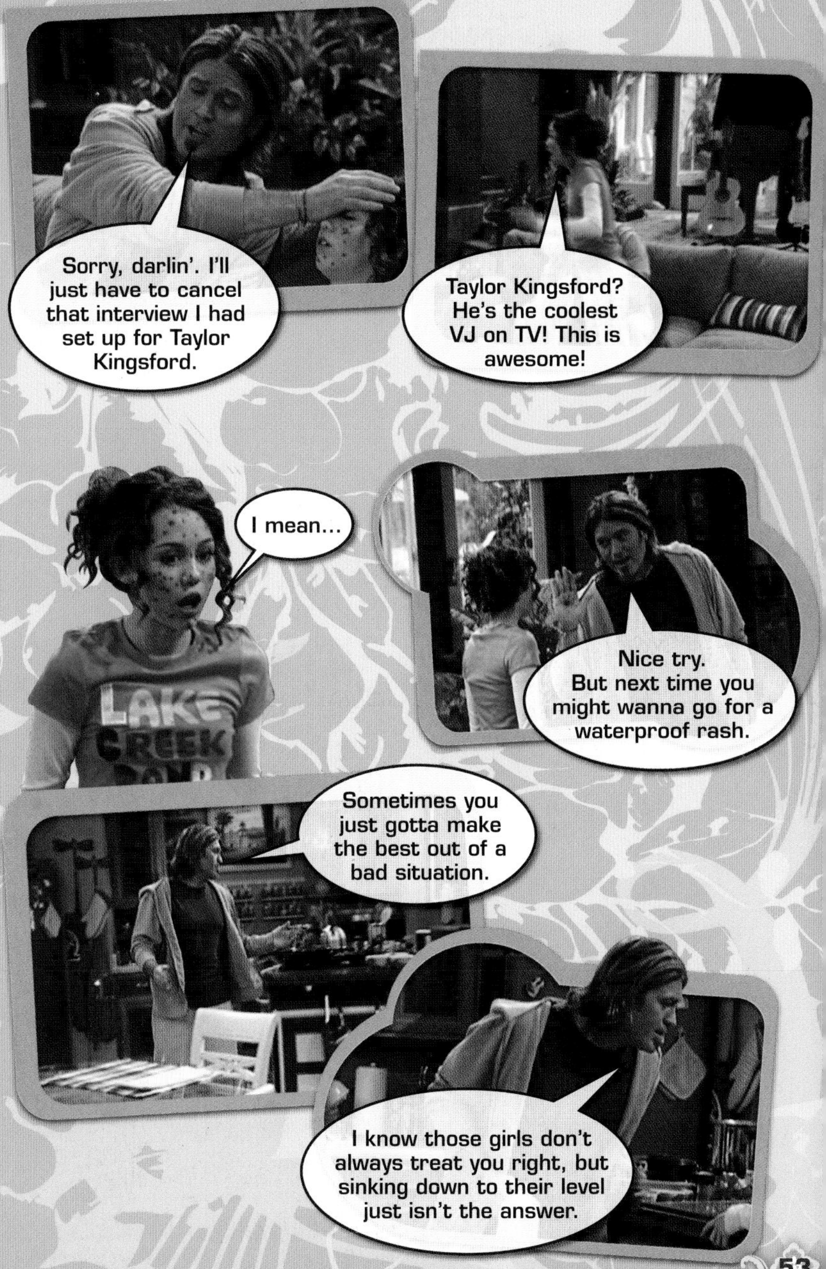
Sorry, darlin'. I'll just have to cancel that interview I had set up for Taylor Kingsford.
Taylor Kingsford? He's the coolest VJ on TV! This is awesome!
I mean...
Nice try. But next time you might wanna go for a waterproof rash.
Sometimes you just gotta make the best out of a bad situation.
I know those girls don't always treat you right, but sinking down to their level just isn't the answer.

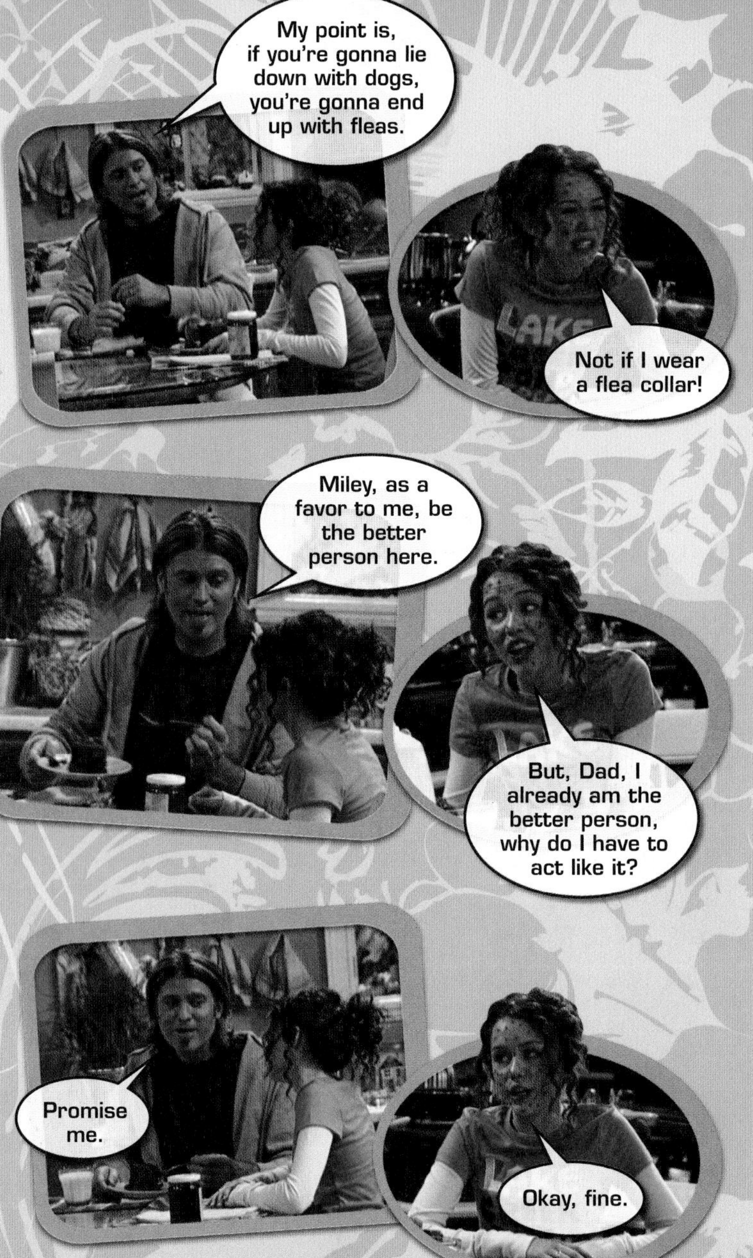
My point is, if you're gonna lie down with dogs, you're gonna end up with fleas.
Not if I wear a flea collar!
Miley, as a favor to me, be the better person here.
But, Dad, I already am the better person, why do I have to act like it?
Promise me.
Okay, fine.

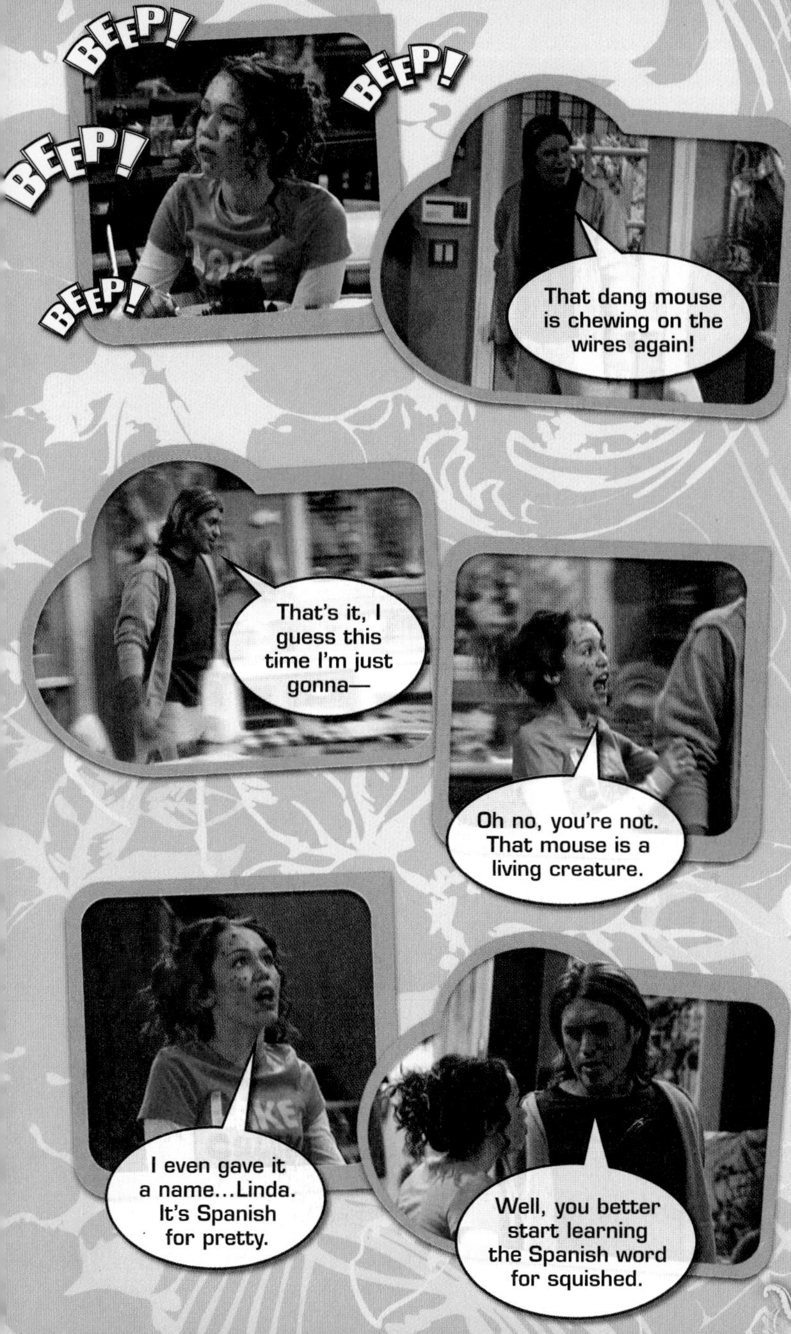
BEEP!
BEEP!
BEEP!
BEEP!
That dang mouse is chewing on the wires again!
That's it, I guess this time I'm just gonna—
Oh no, you're not. That mouse is a living creature.
I even gave it a name...Linda. It's Spanish for pretty.
Well, you better start learning the Spanish word for squished.

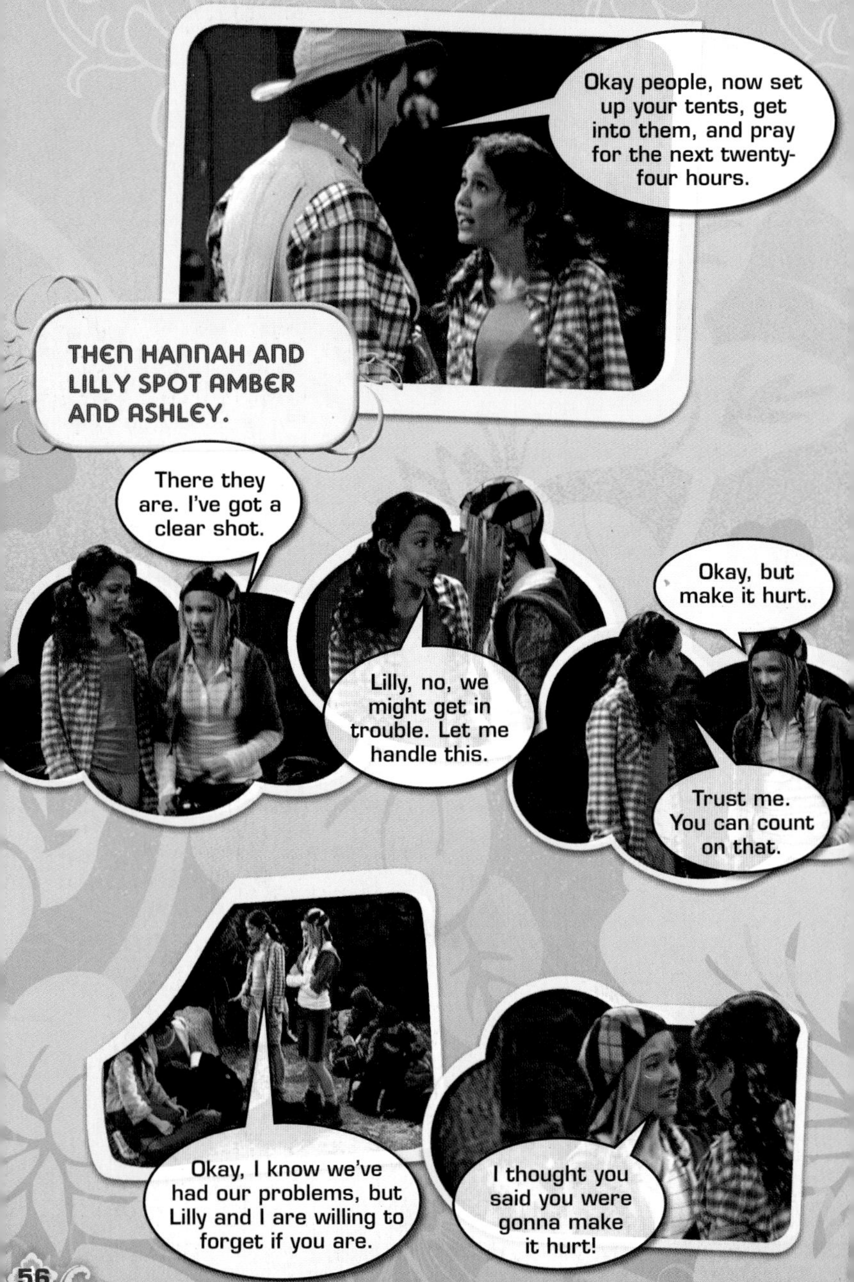
Okay people, now set up your tents, get into them, and pray for the next twenty-four hours.
THEN HANNAH AND LILLY SPOT AMBER AND ASHLEY.
There they are. I've got a clear shot.
Lilly, no, we might get in trouble. Let me handle this.
Okay, but make it hurt.
Trust me. You can count on that.
Okay, I know we've had our problems, but Lilly and I are willing to forget if you are.
I thought you said you were gonna make it hurt!

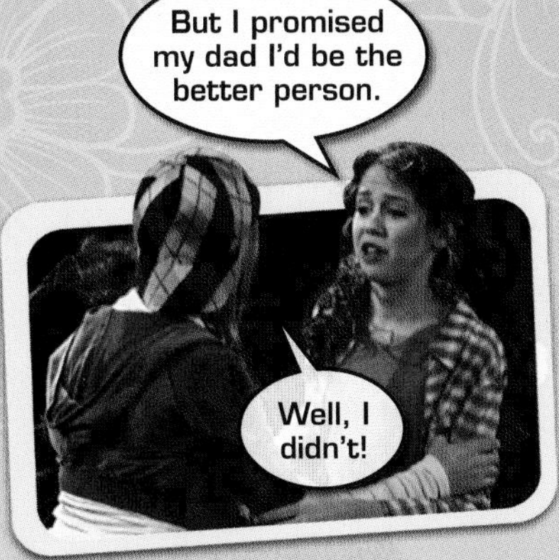
But I promised my dad I'd be the better person.
Well, I didn't!

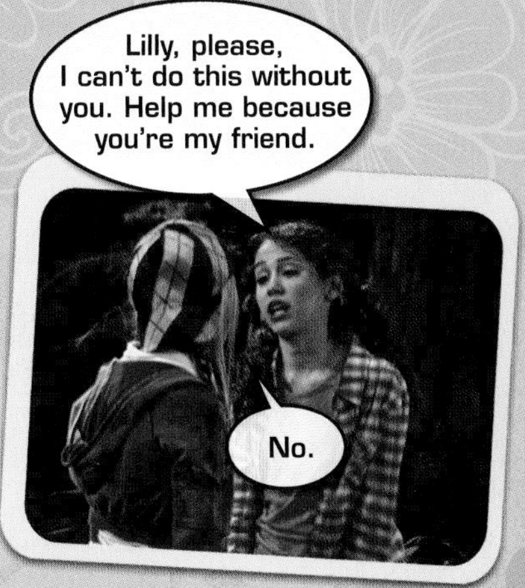
Lilly, please, I can't do this without you. Help me because you're my friend.
No.

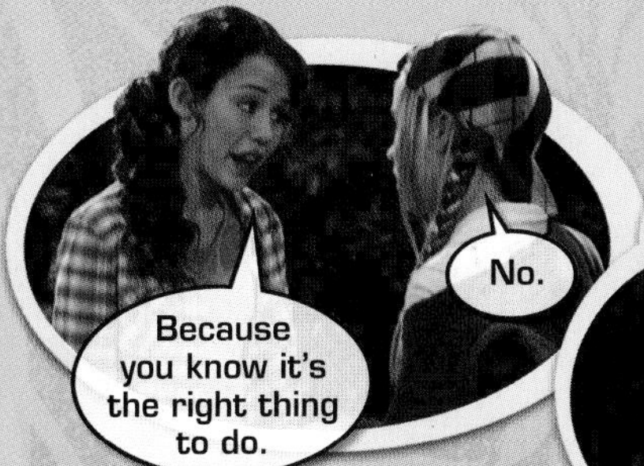
No.
Because you know it's the right thing to do.

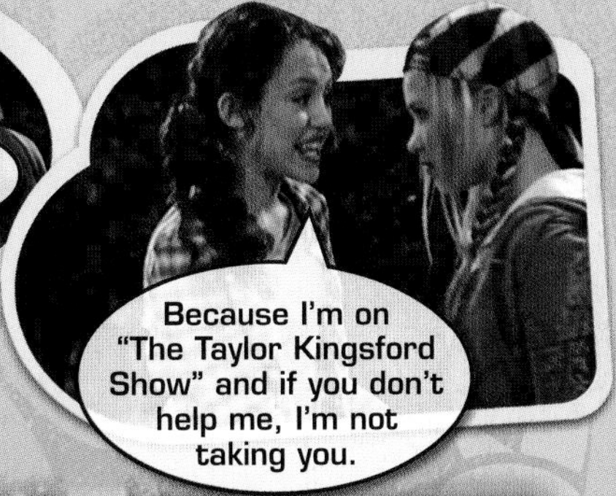
Because I'm on "The Taylor Kingsford Show" and if you don't help me, I'm not taking you.

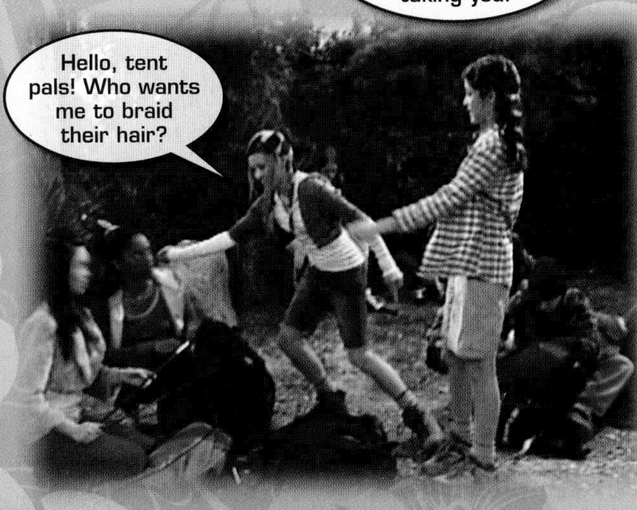
Hello, tent pals! Who wants me to braid their hair?

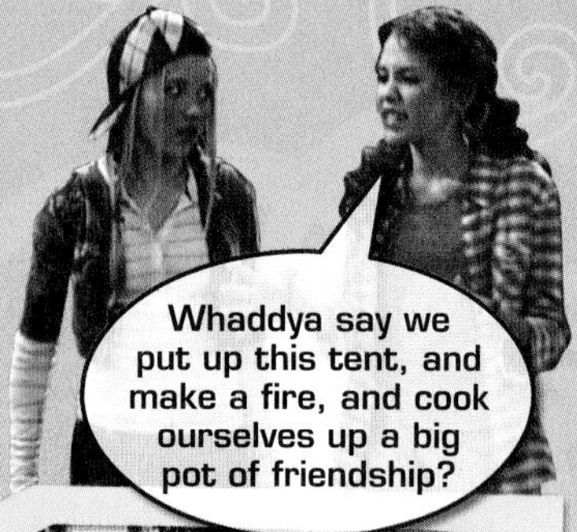
Whaddya say we put up this tent, and make a fire, and cook ourselves up a big pot of friendship?

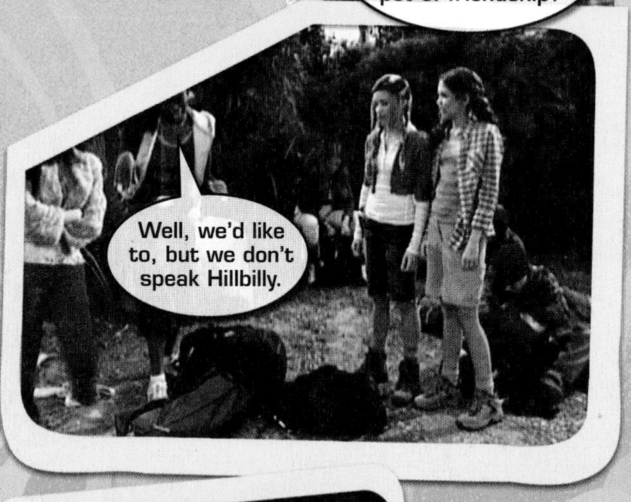
Well, we'd like to, but we don't speak Hillbilly.

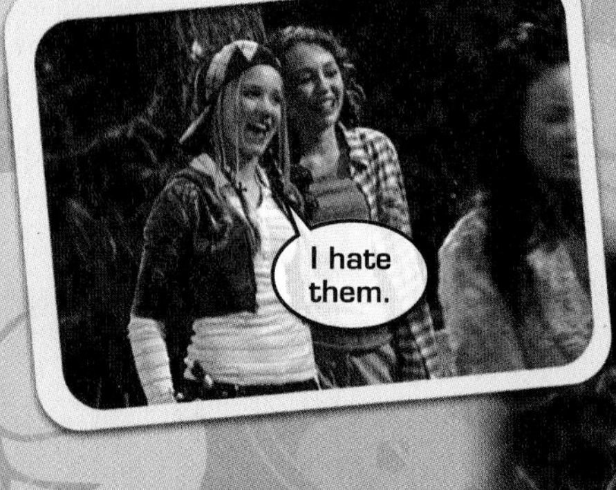
I hate them.

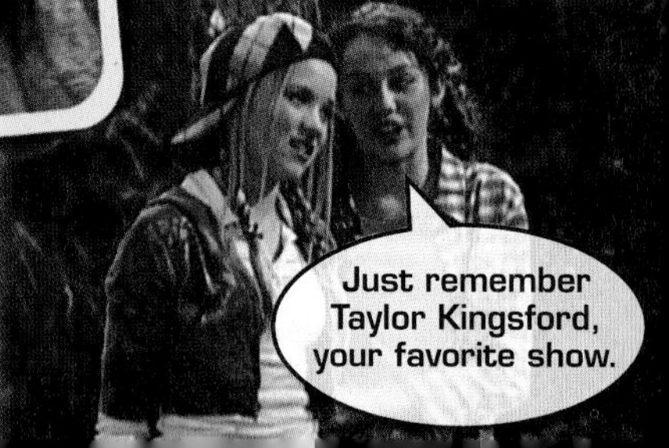
Just remember Taylor Kingsford, your favorite show.

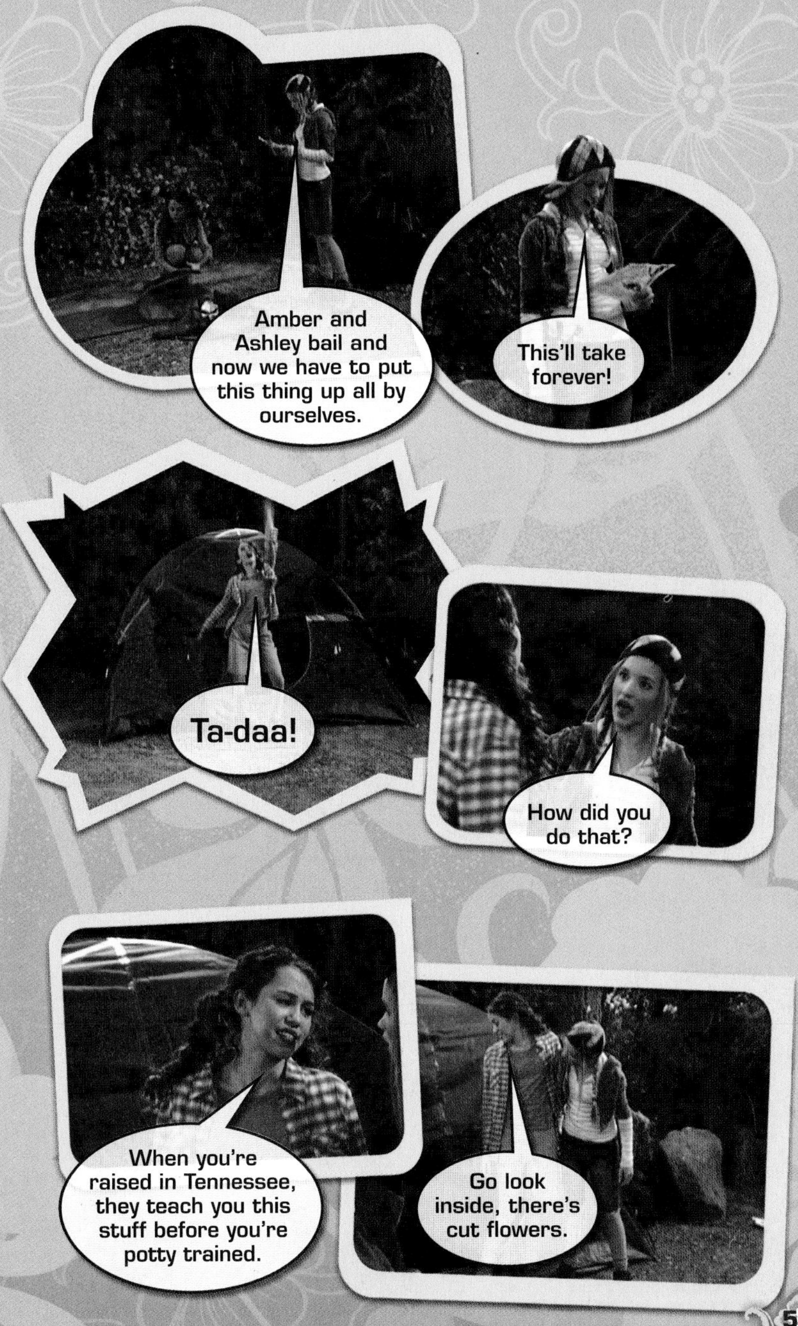
Amber and Ashley bail and now we have to put this thing up all by ourselves.
This'll take forever!
Ta-daa!
How did you do that?
When you're raised in Tennessee, they teach you this stuff before you're potty trained.
Go look inside, there's cut flowers.

BACK AT MILEY'S HOUSE...

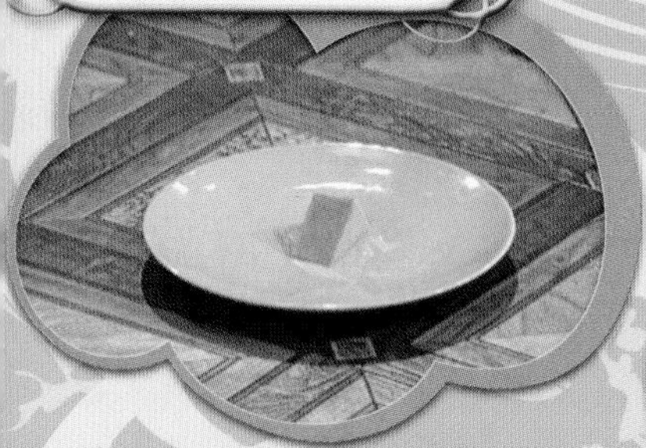

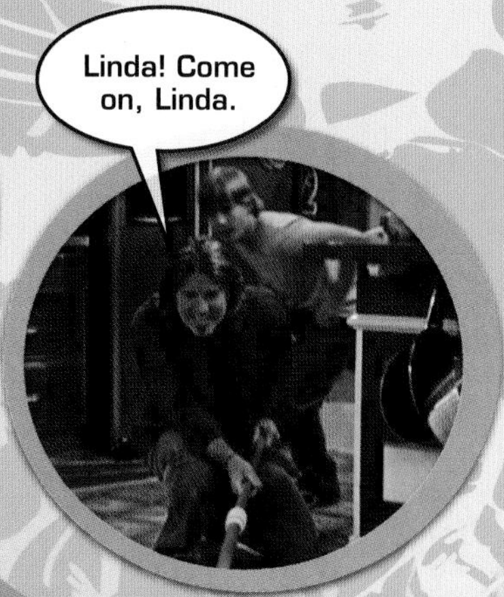
Linda! Come on, Linda.

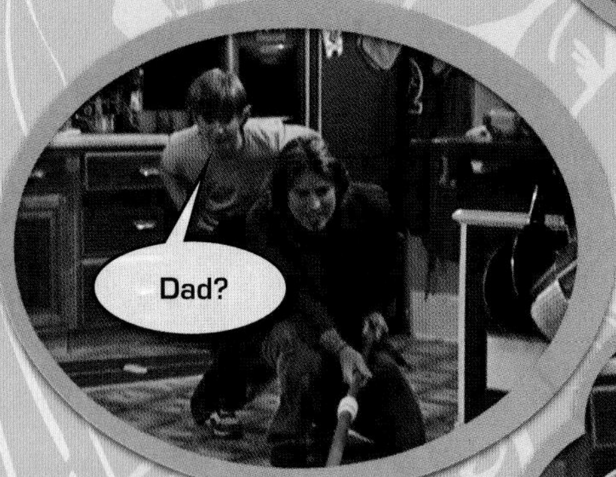
Dad?

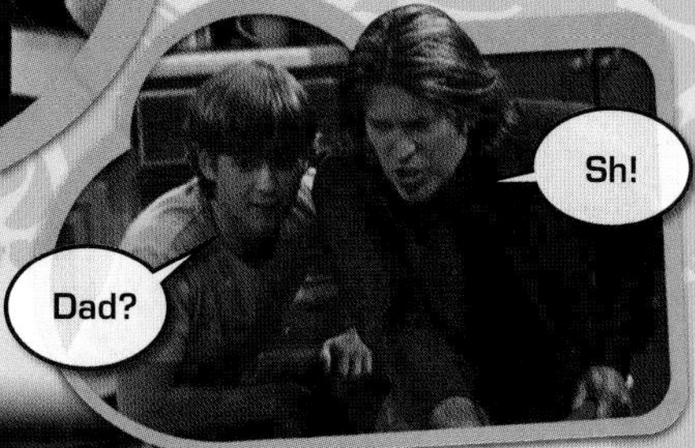
Dad?
Sh!

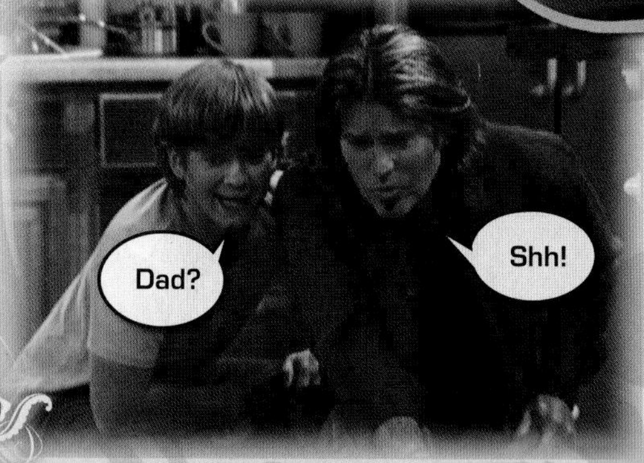
Dad?
Shh!

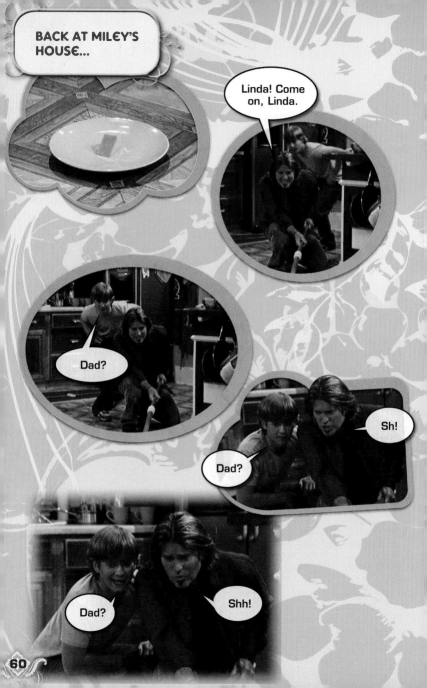

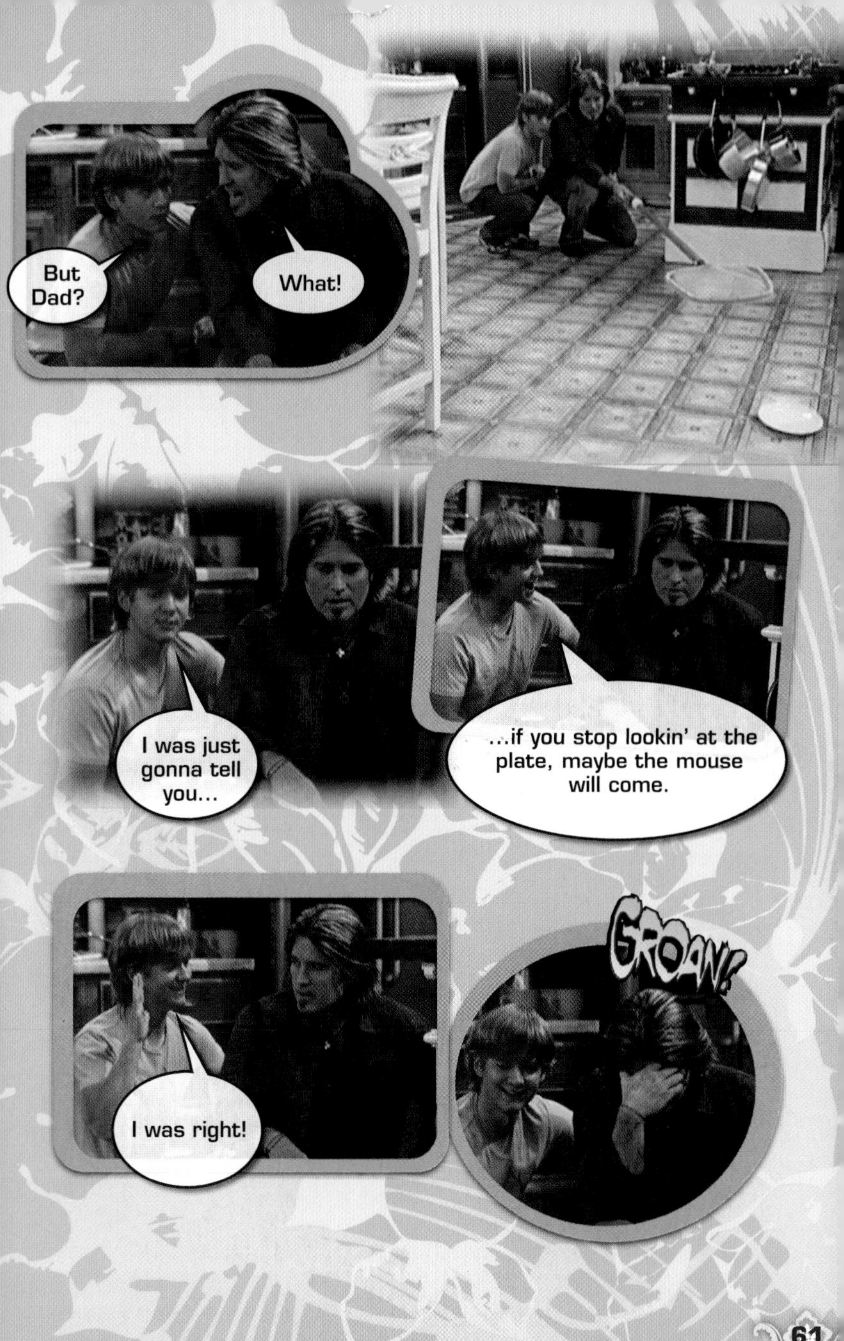
But Dad?
What!
I was just gonna tell you...
...if you stop lookin' at the plate, maybe the mouse will come.
I was right!
GROAN!

MEANWHILE, BACK AT CAMP, ASHLEY AND AMBER TRY TO TAKE CREDIT FOR SETTING UP THE TENT.

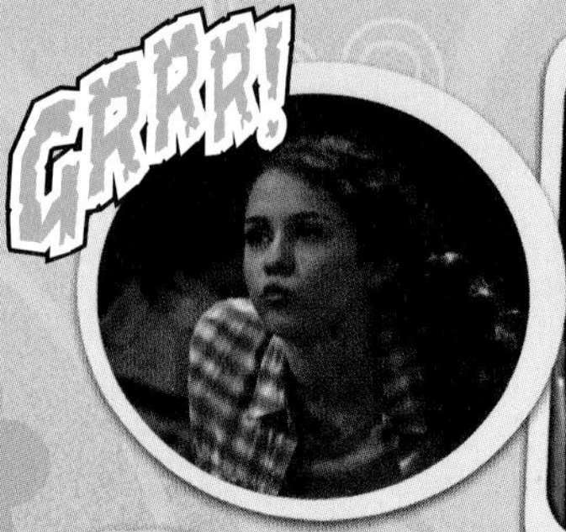
GRRR!

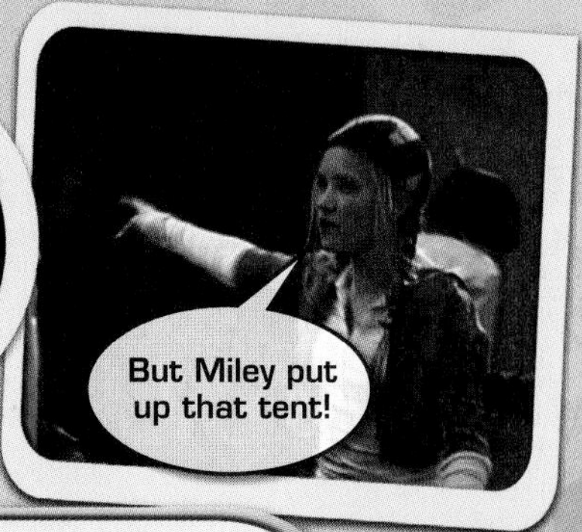
But Miley put up that tent!

AMBER AND ASHLEY HAVE THE NERVE TO SAY ALL THEY WANTED TO DO WAS "PUT UP A TENT, MAKE A FIRE, AND COOK UP A BIG POT OF FRIENDSHIP!"

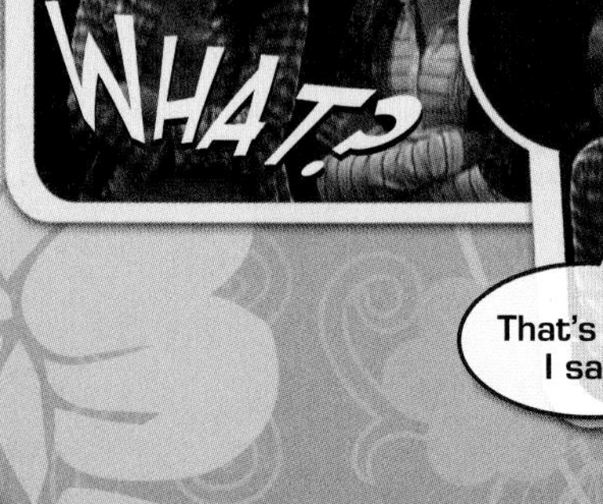
WHAT?

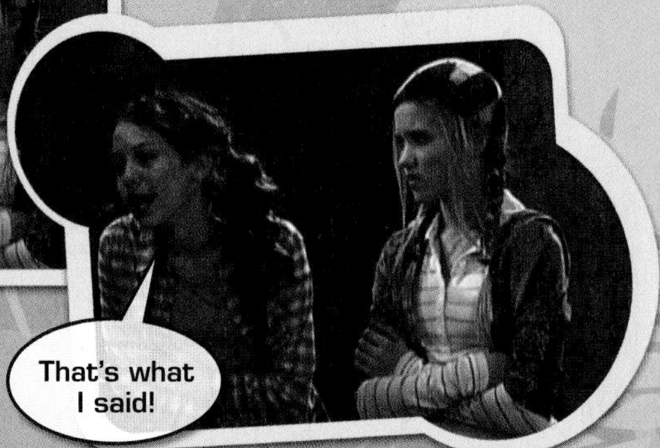
That's what I said!

MR. PICKER ASKS THEM TO APOLOGIZE TO EACH OTHER.

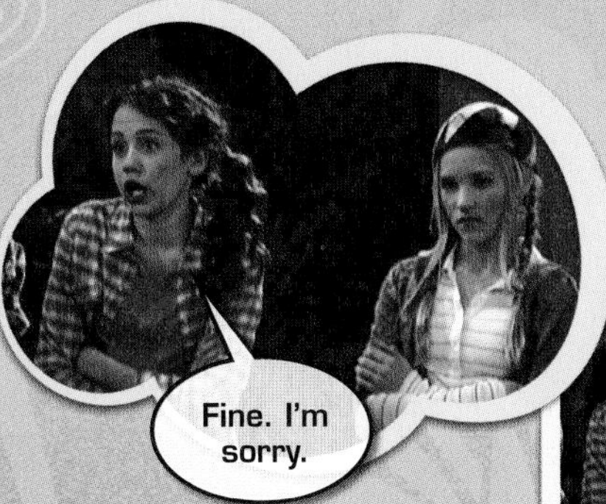
Fine. I'm sorry.

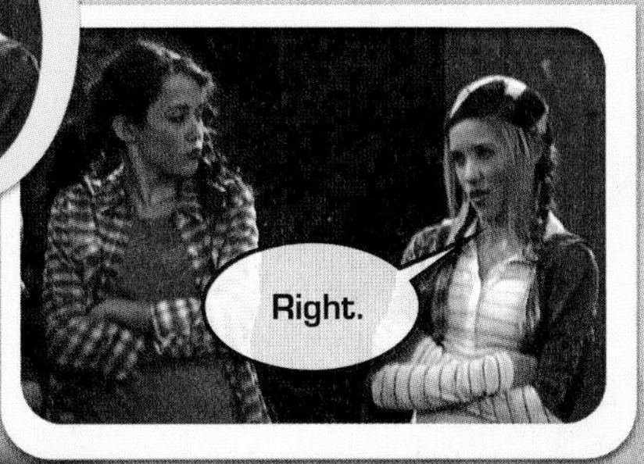
Right.

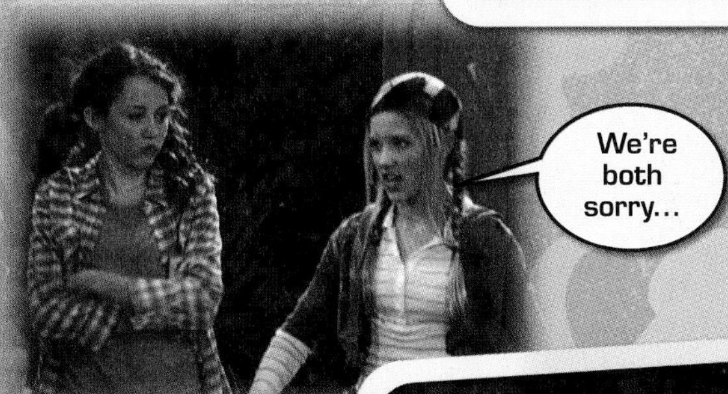
We're both sorry...

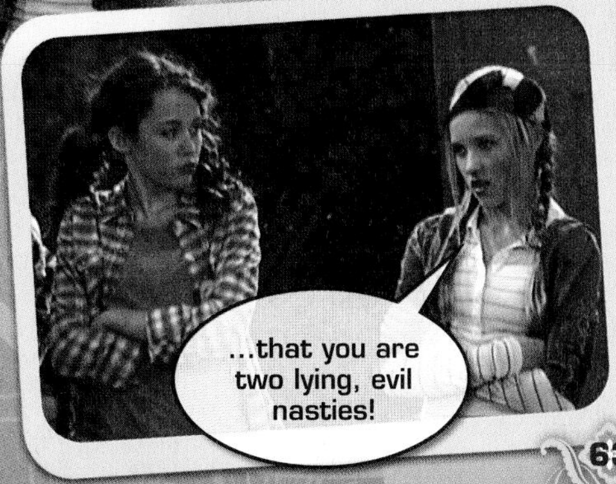
...that you are two lying, evil nasties!

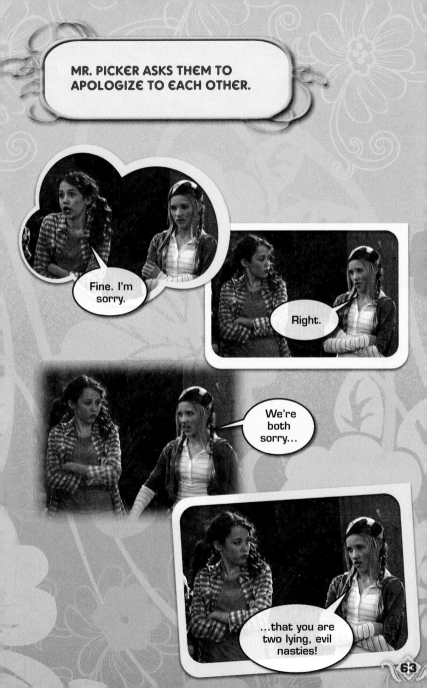

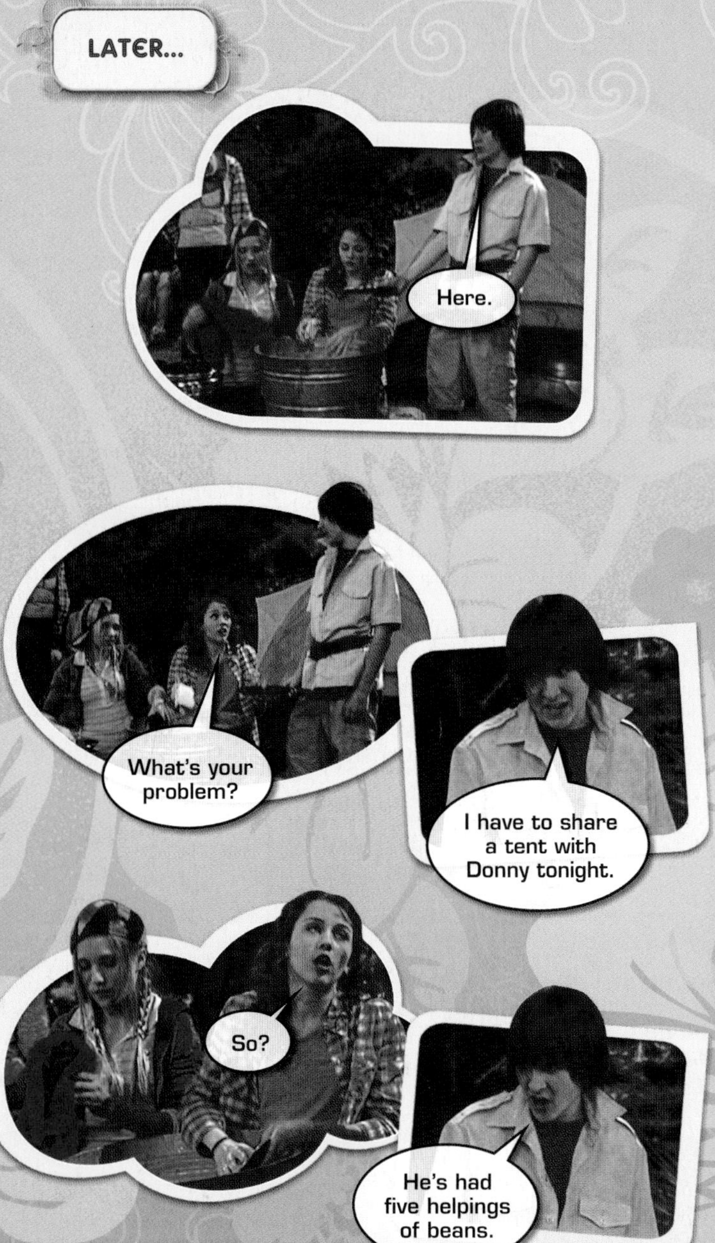
LATER...
Here.
What's your problem?
I have to share a tent with Donny tonight.
So?
He's had five helpings of beans.

AFTER ASHLEY AND AMBER MOCK MILEY AND LILLY FOR HAVING TO WASH ALL THE DISHES, MILEY AND LILLY DECIDE TO TAKE ACTION!

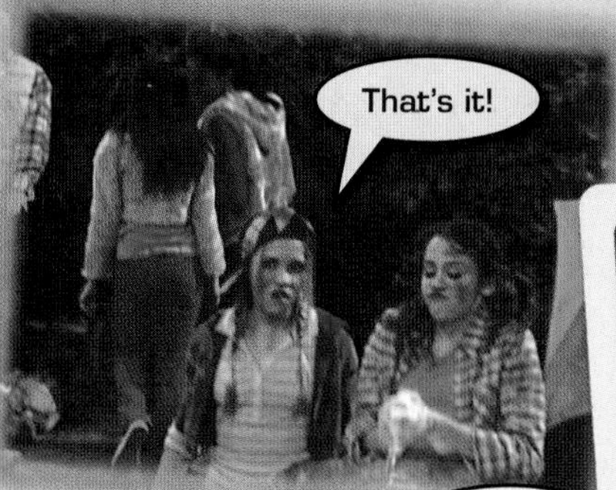
That's it!

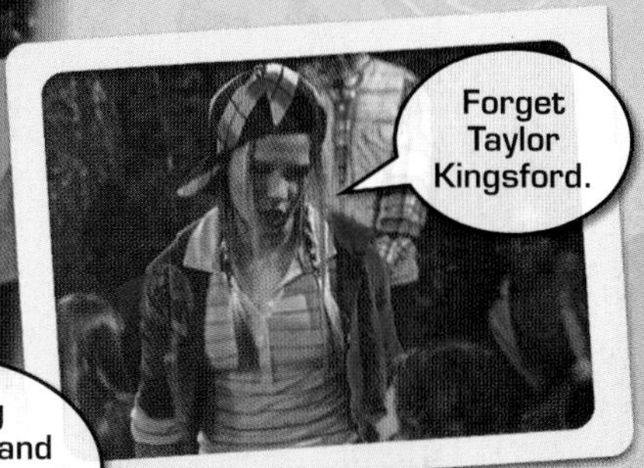
Forget Taylor Kingsford.

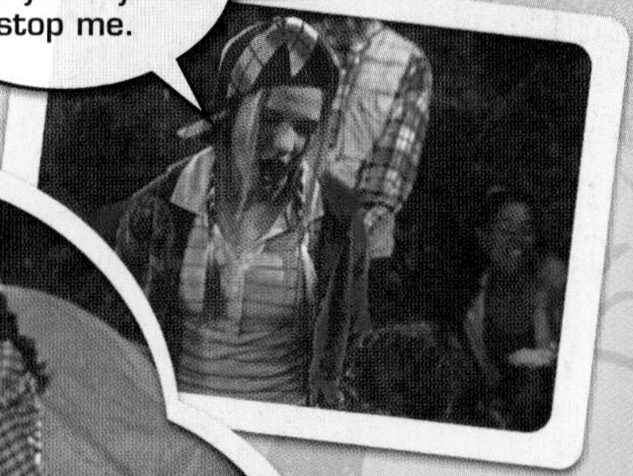
I'm going after them and don't you try and stop me.

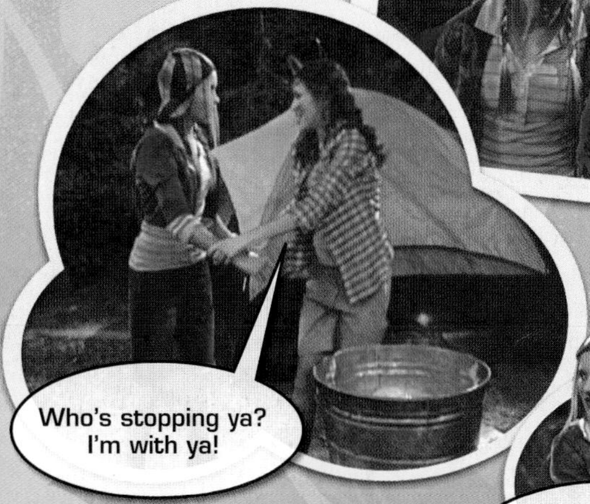
Who's stopping ya? I'm with ya!

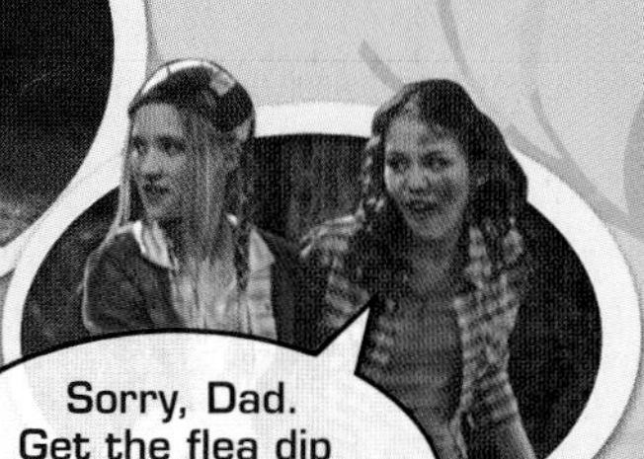
Sorry, Dad. Get the flea dip ready, 'cause tonight I'm lyin' down with the dogs.

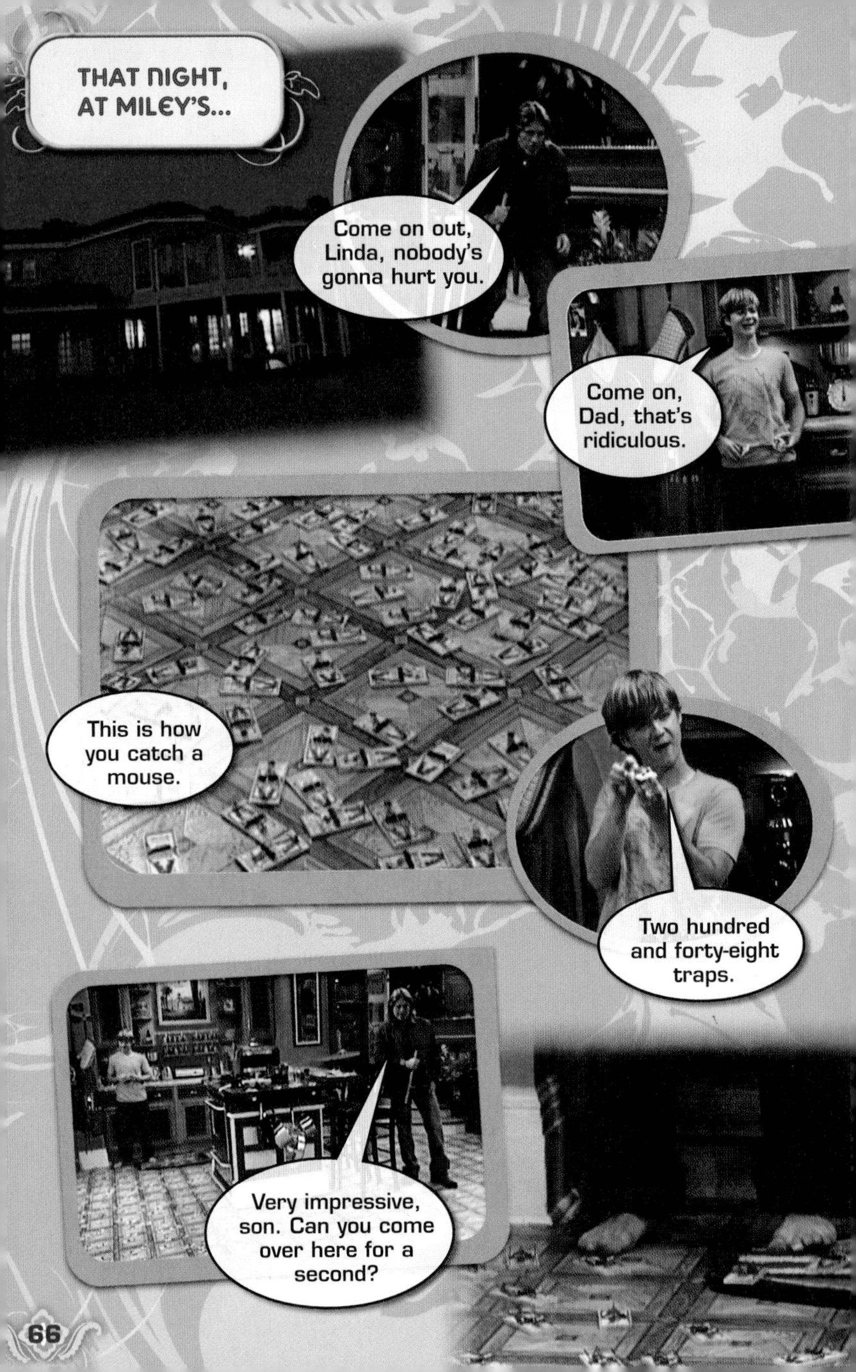
THAT NIGHT, AT MILEY'S...
Come on out, Linda, nobody's gonna hurt you.
Come on, Dad, that's ridiculous.
This is how you catch a mouse.
Two hundred and forty-eight traps.
Very impressive, son. Can you come over here for a second?

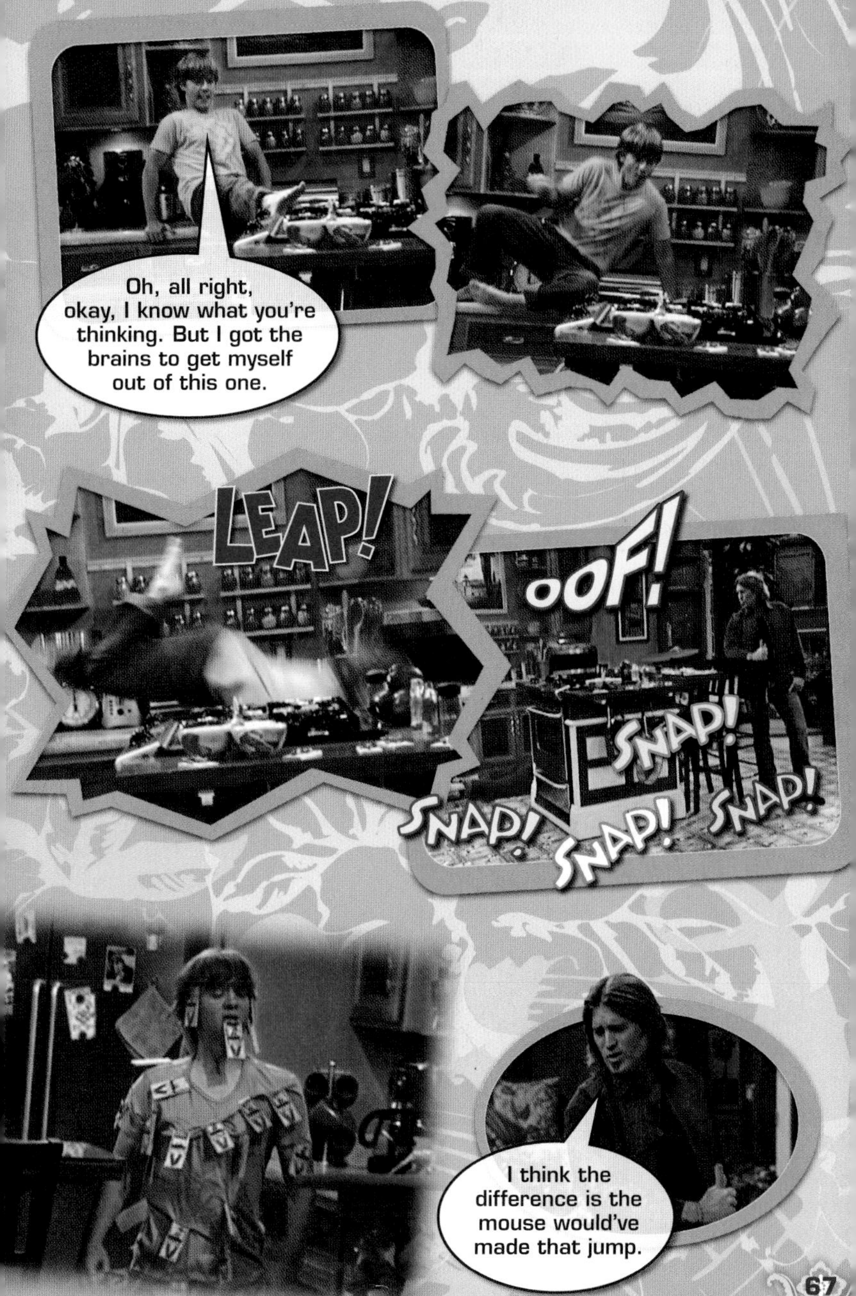
Oh, all right, okay, I know what you're thinking. But I got the brains to get myself out of this one.
LEAP!
OOF!
SNAP!
SNAP!
SNAP!
SNAP!
I think the difference is the mouse would've made that jump.

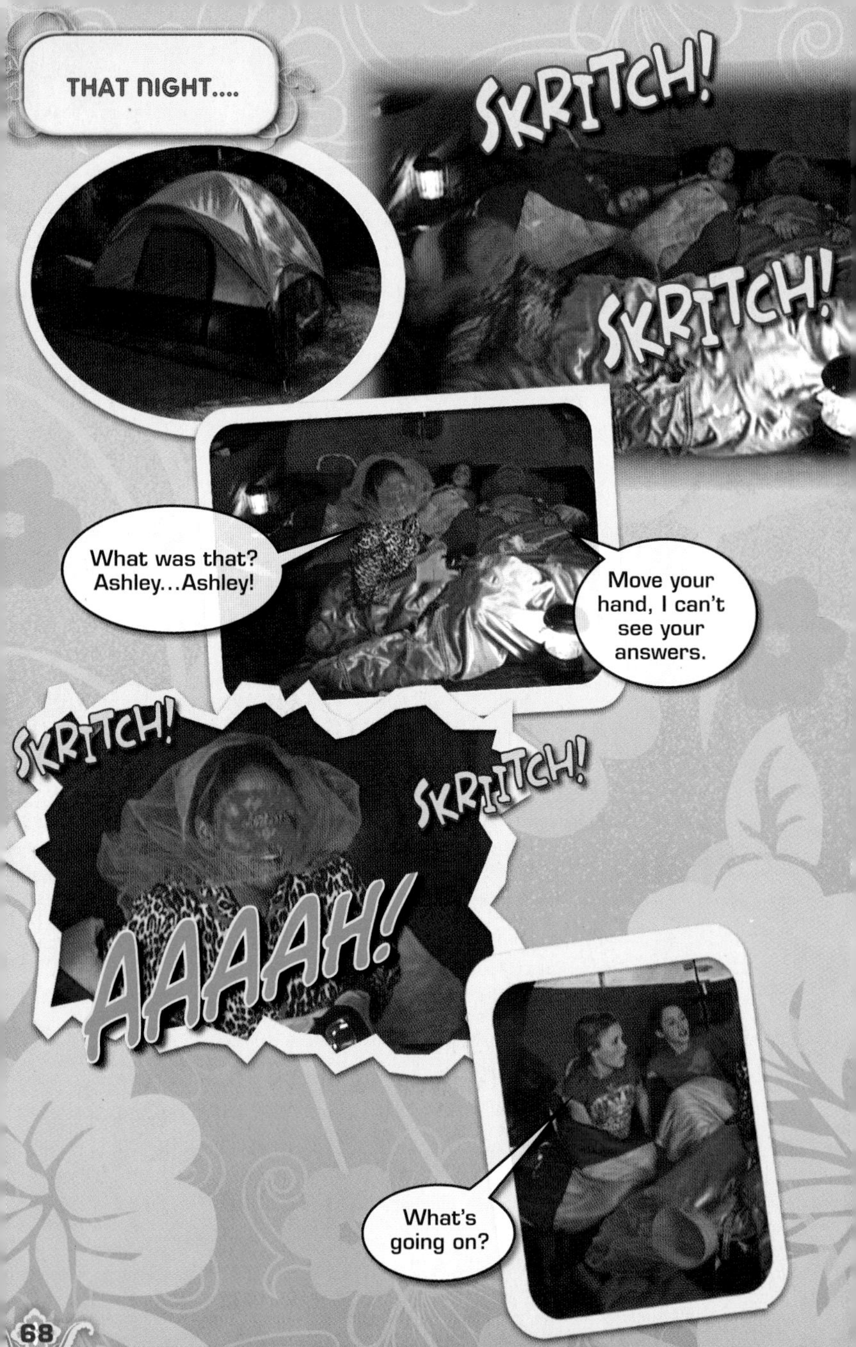
THAT NIGHT....
SKRITCH!
SKRITCH!
What was that? Ashley...Ashley!
Move your hand, I can't see your answers.
SKRITCH!
SKRITCH!
AAAAH!
What's going on?

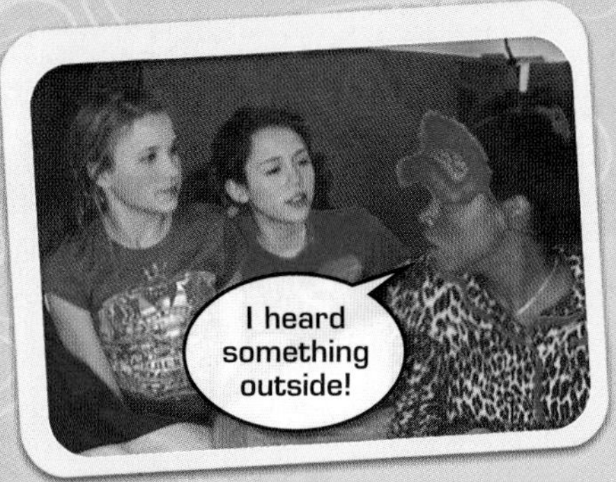
I heard something outside!

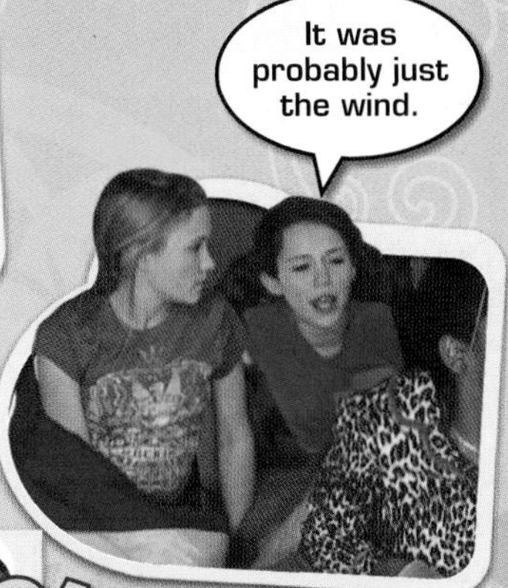
It was probably just the wind.

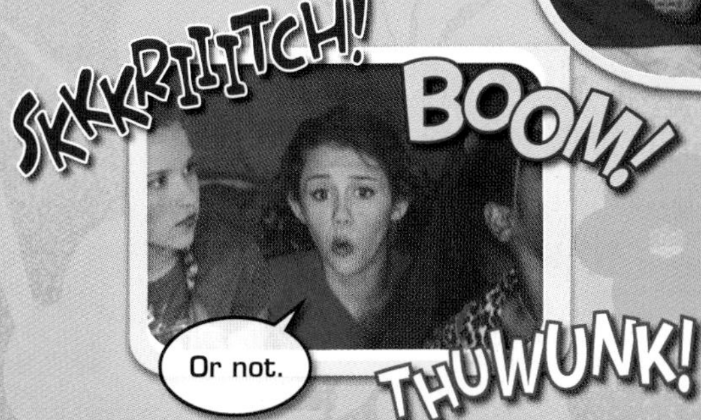
SKKRIIIITCH!
BOOM!
Or not.
THUWUNK!

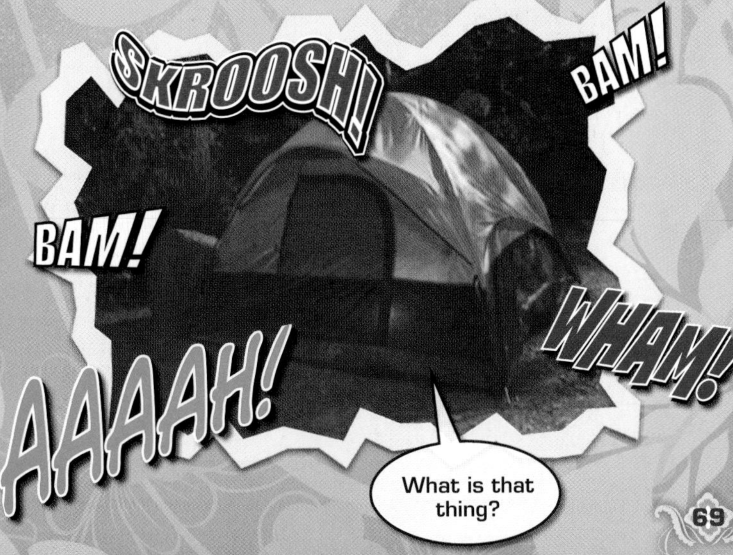
SKROOSH!
BAM!
BAM!
WHAM!
AAAAH!
What is that thing?

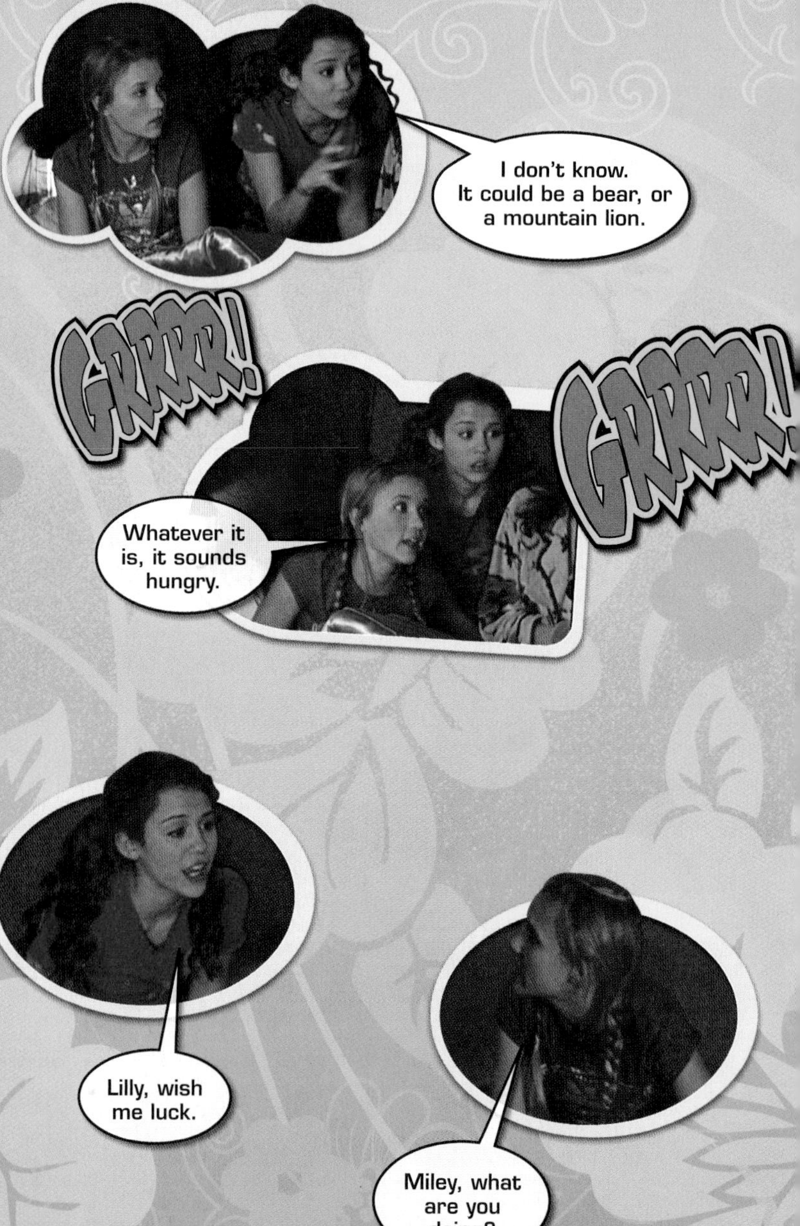
I don't know.
It could be a bear, or a mountain lion.
GRRRR!
GRRRR!
Whatever it is, it sounds hungry.
Lilly, wish me luck.
Miley, what are you doing?

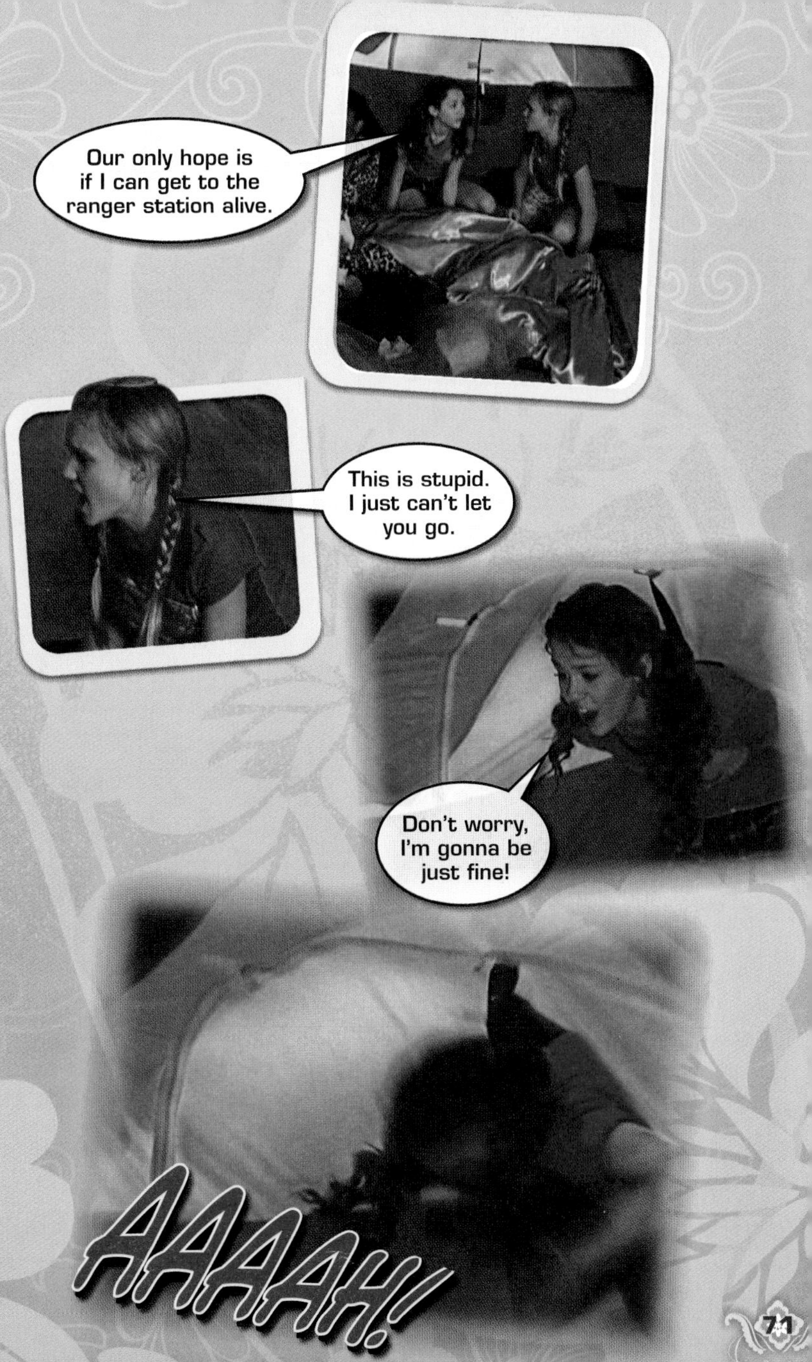
Our only hope is if I can get to the ranger station alive.
This is stupid. I just can't let you go.
Don't worry, I'm gonna be just fine!
AAAAH!

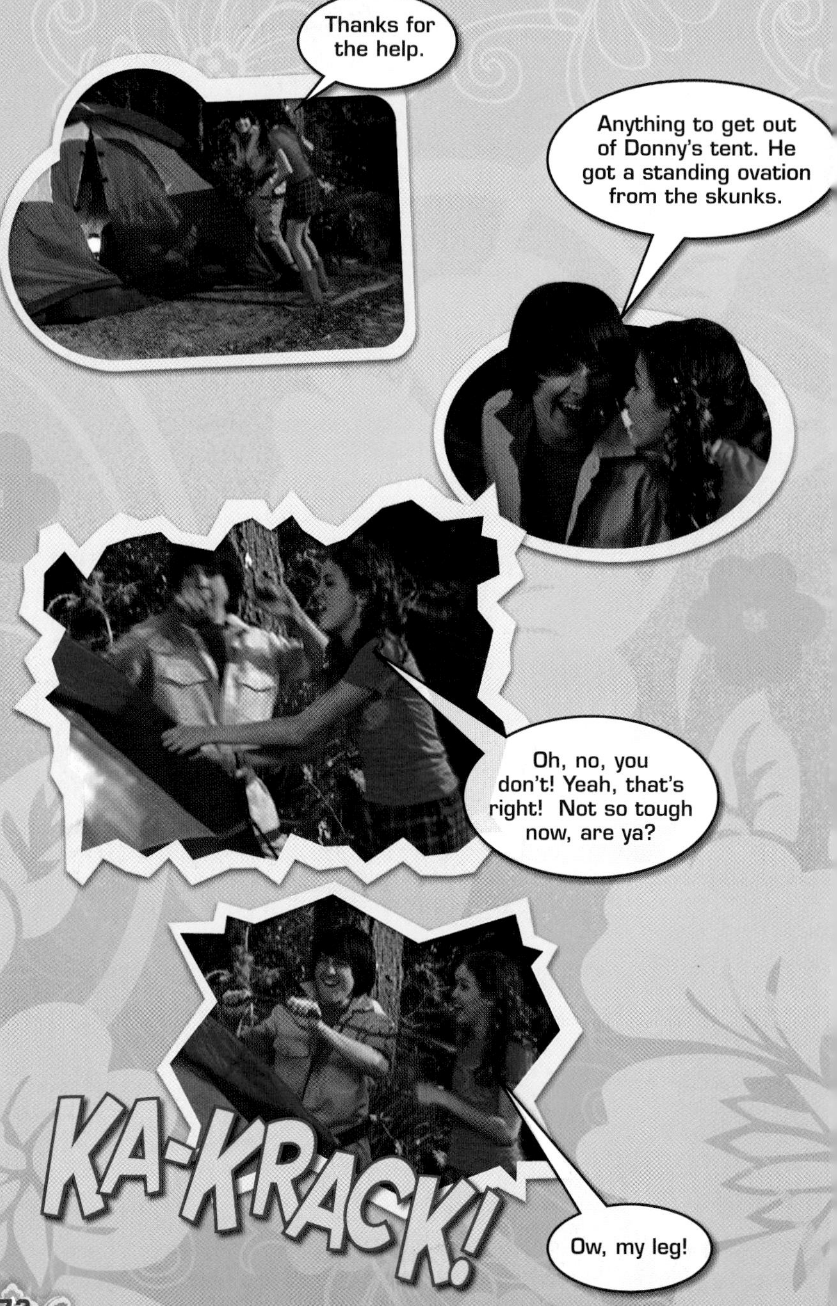
Thanks for the help.
Anything to get out of Donny's tent. He got a standing ovation from the skunks.
Oh, no, you don't! Yeah, that's right! Not so tough now, are ya?
KA-KRACK!
Ow, my leg!

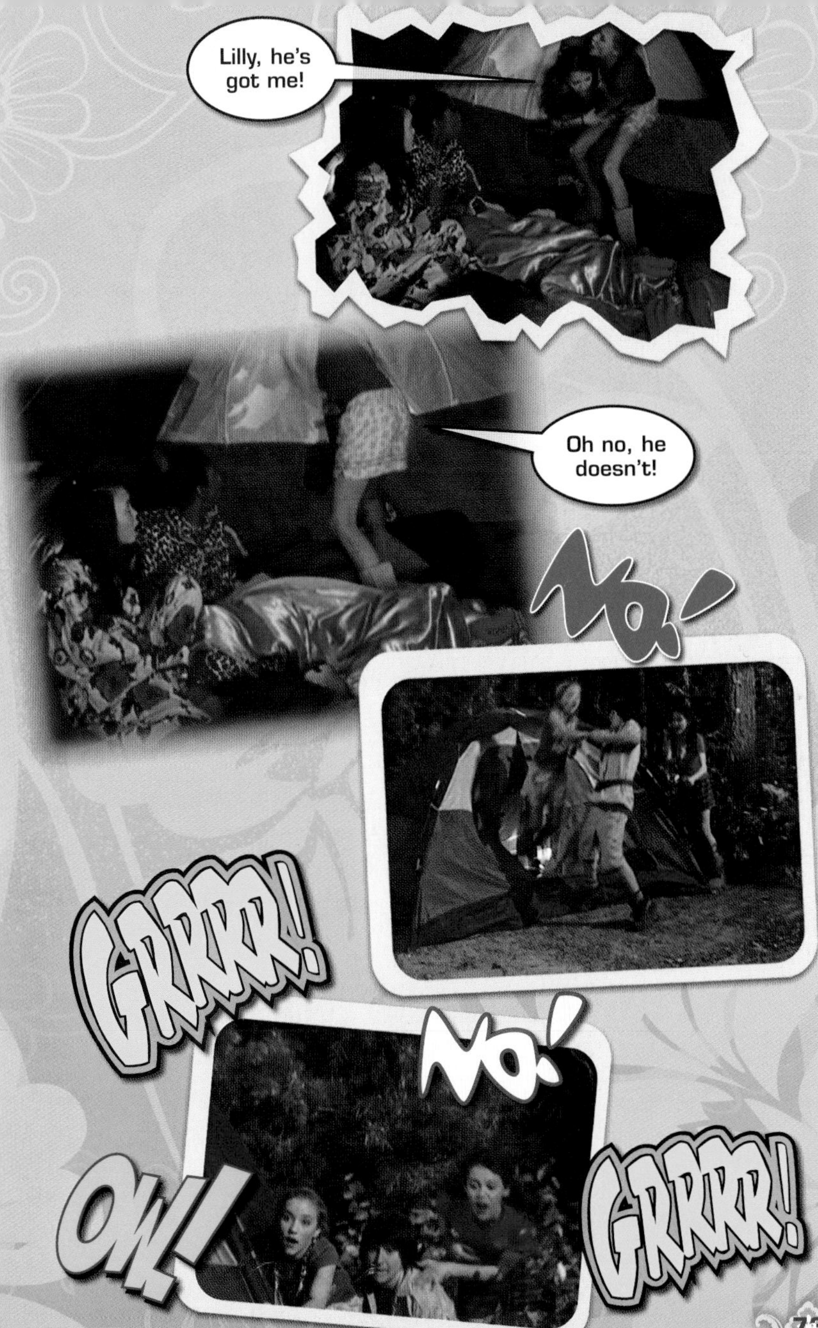
Lilly, he's got me!
Oh no, he doesn't!
No!
GRRRR!
No!
OW!
GRRRR!

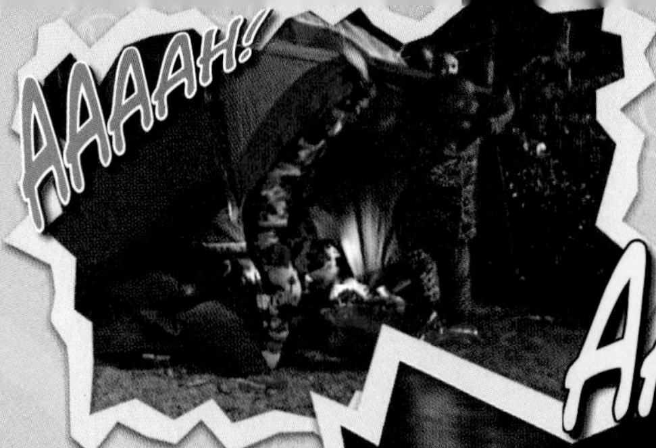
AAAAH!

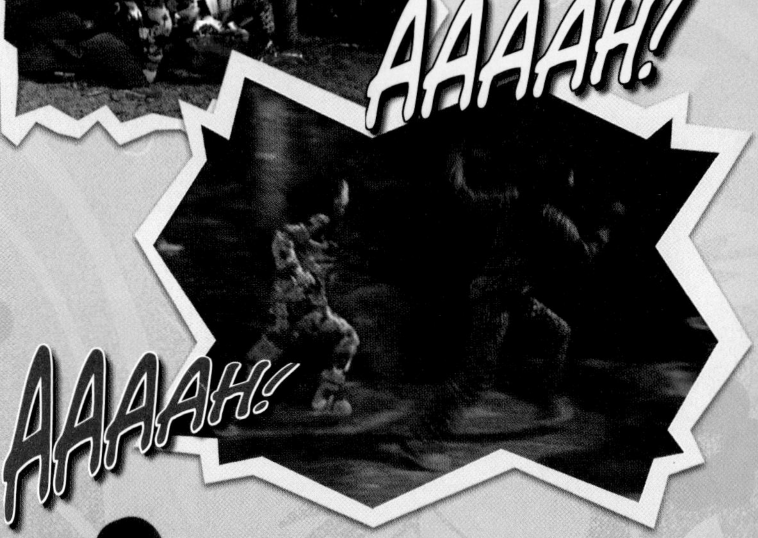
AAAAH!
AAAAH!

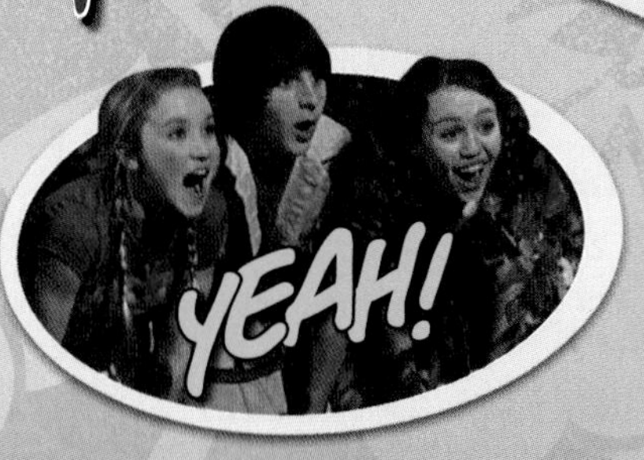
YEAH!

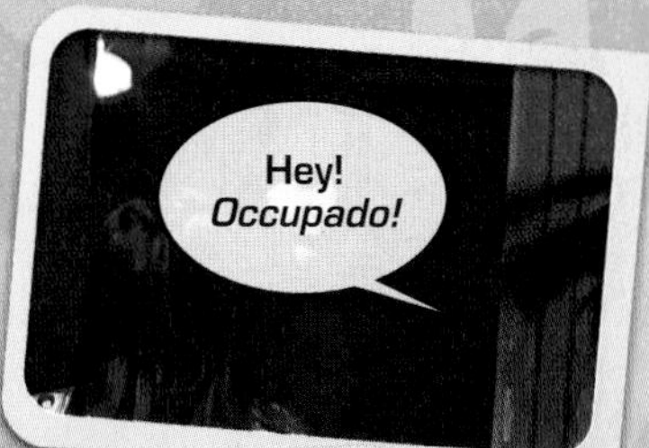
Hey!
Occupado!

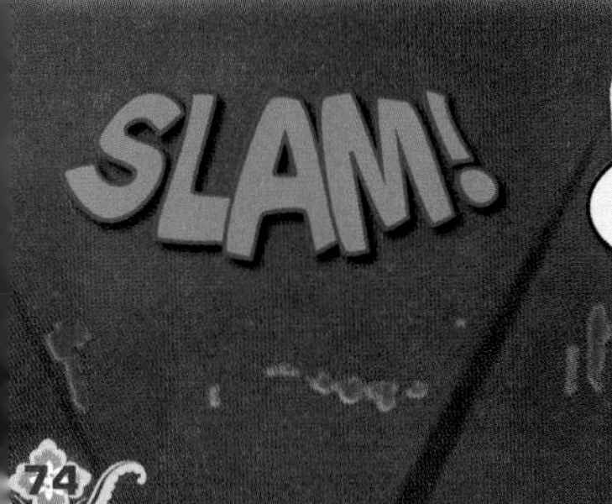
SLAM!

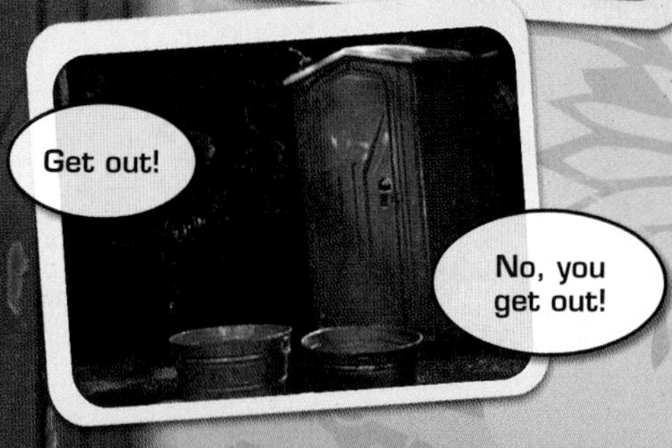
Get out!
No, you get out!

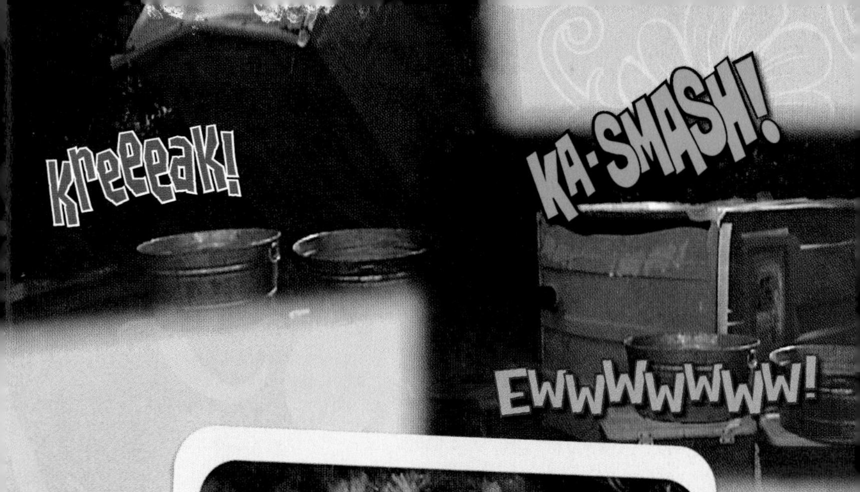
Kreeeak!
KA-SMASH!
EWWWWWWW!

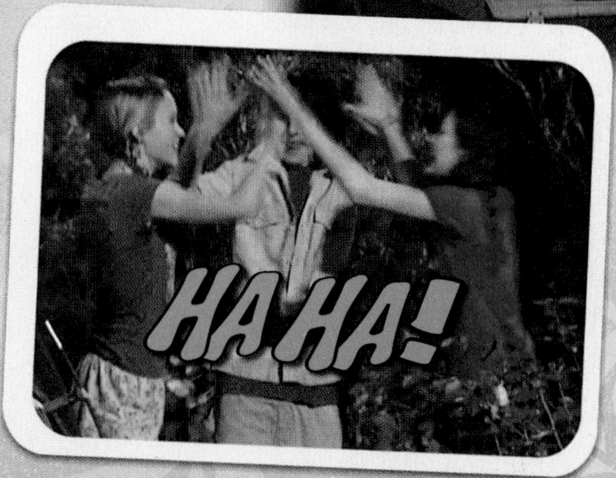
HA HA!

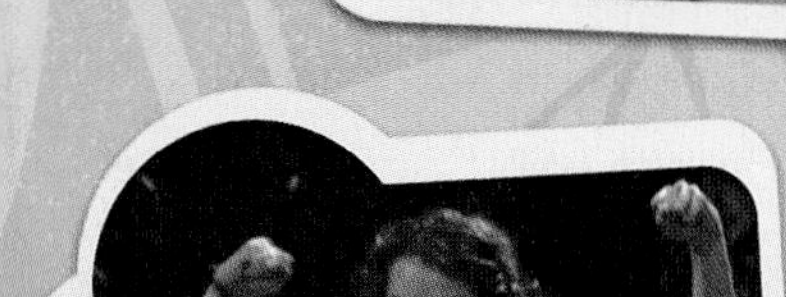
Yeah! Looks like Daddy was wrong.

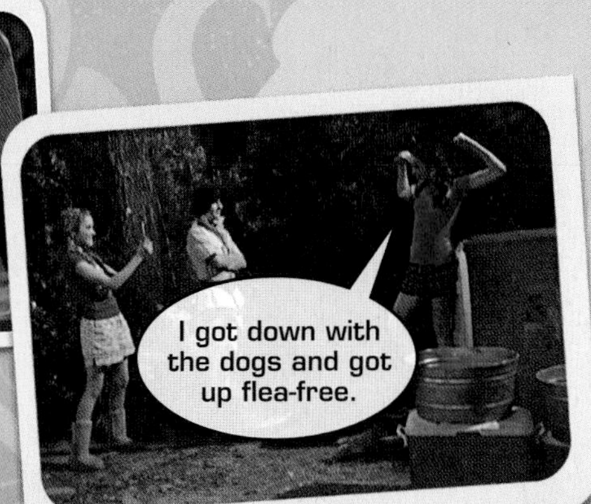
I got down with the dogs and got up flea-free.

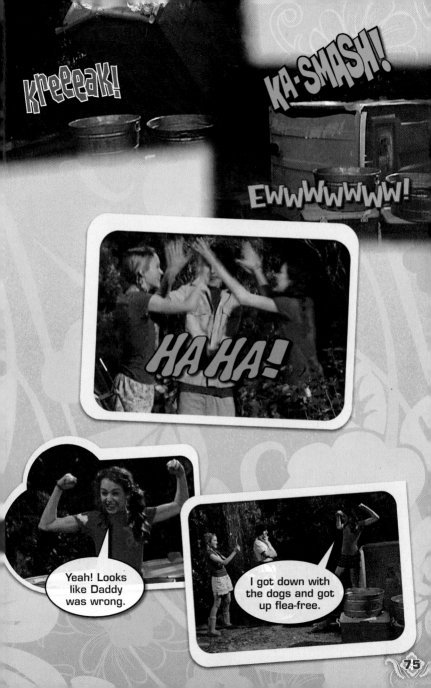

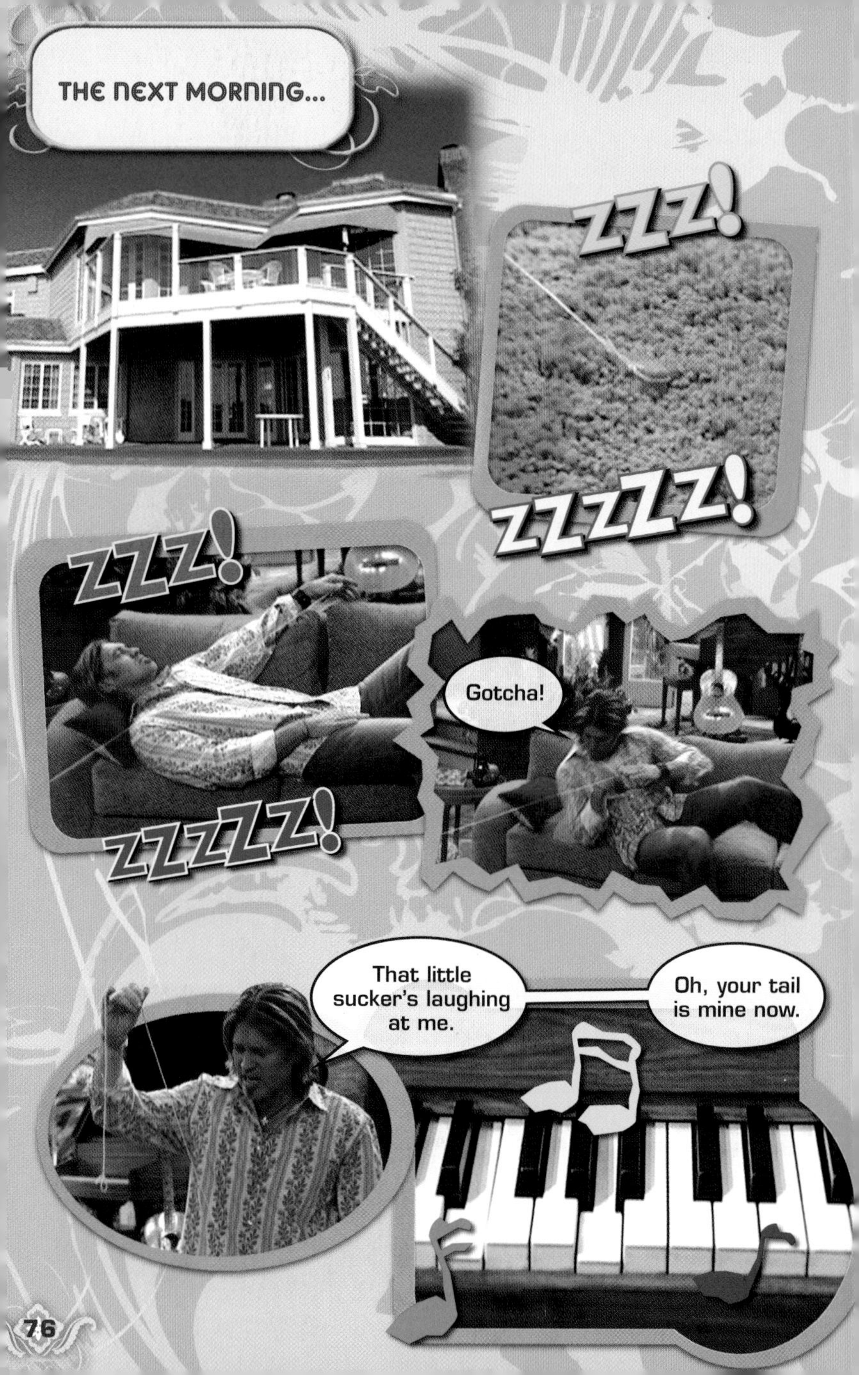
THE NEXT MORNING...
ZZZ!
ZZZZZ!
ZZZ!
ZZZZZ!
Gotcha!
That little sucker's laughing at me.
Oh, your tail is mine now.

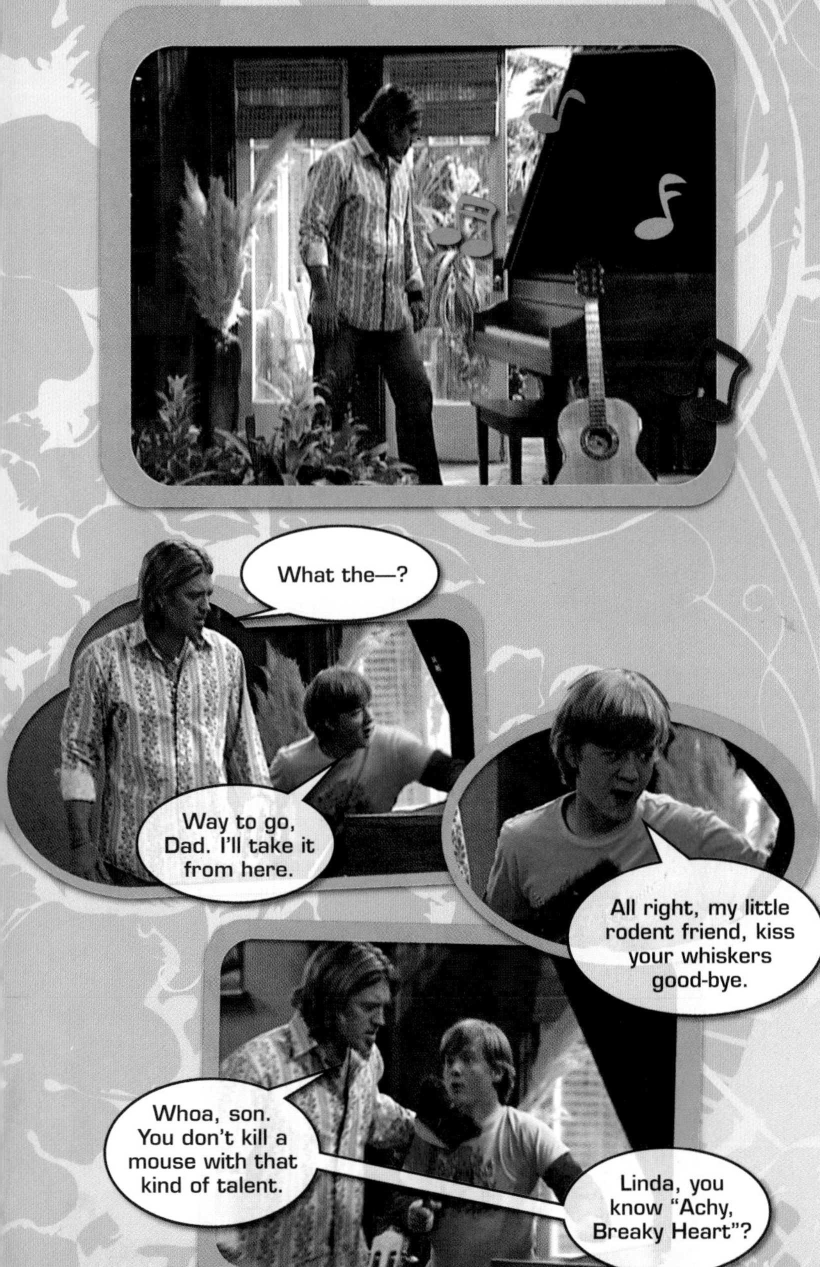
What the—?
Way to go, Dad. I'll take it from here.
All right, my little rodent friend, kiss your whiskers good-bye.
Whoa, son. You don't kill a mouse with that kind of talent.
Linda, you know "Achy, Breaky Heart"?

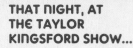

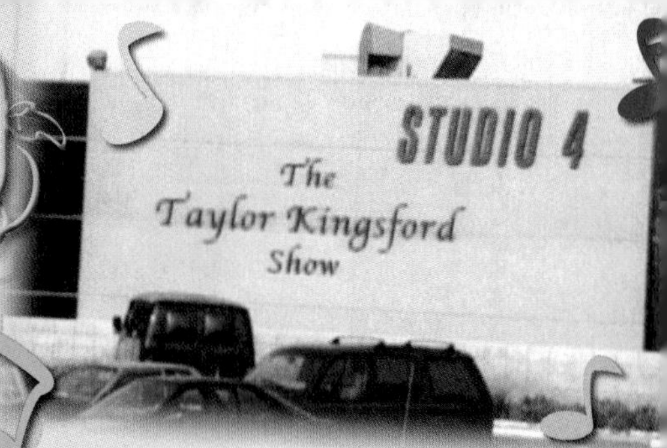
THAT NIGHT, AT THE TAYLOR KINGSFORD SHOW...
STUDIO 4
The Taylor Kingsford Show

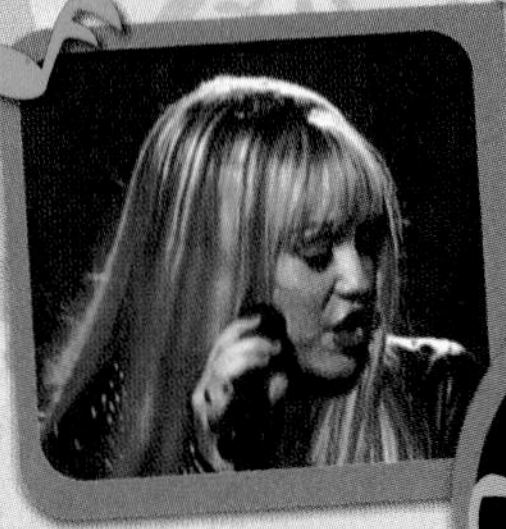

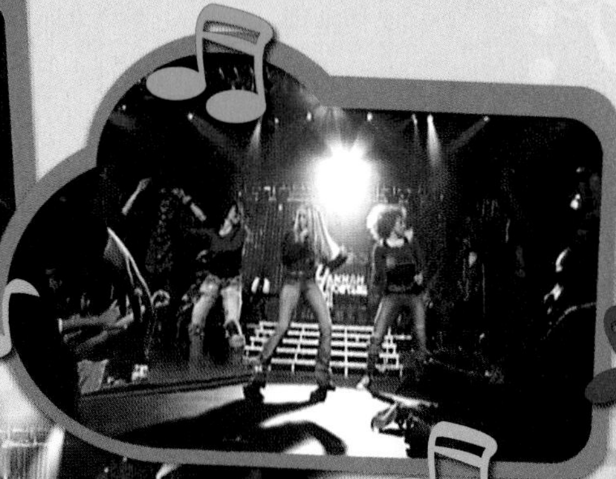

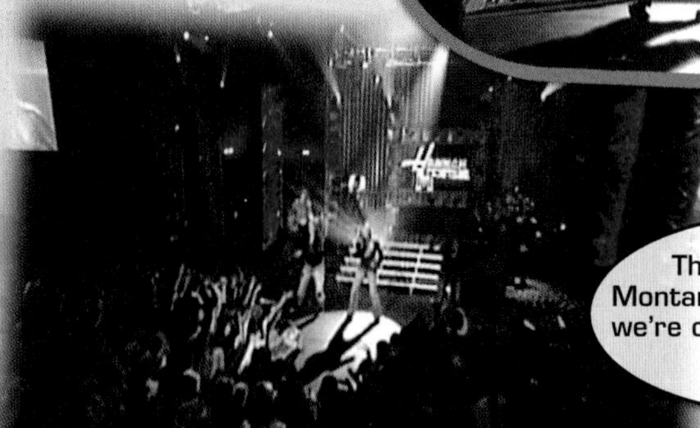
That was Hannah Montana! And in a minute, we're comin' back with the real thing.

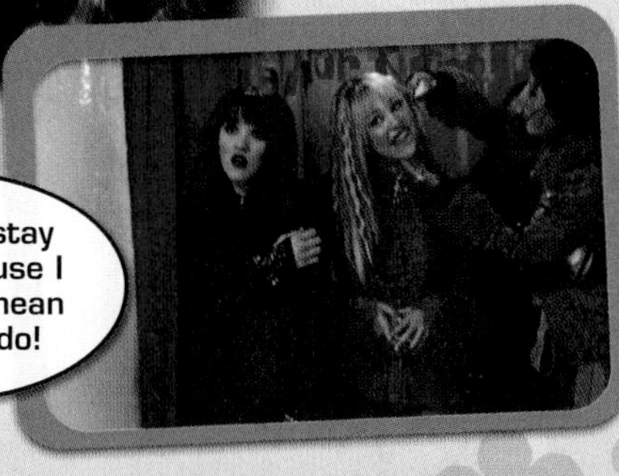
So please stay tuned because I love you! I mean it! I really do!

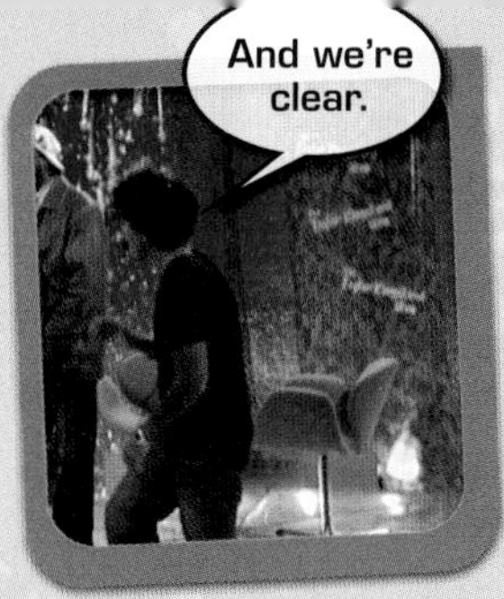
And we're clear.

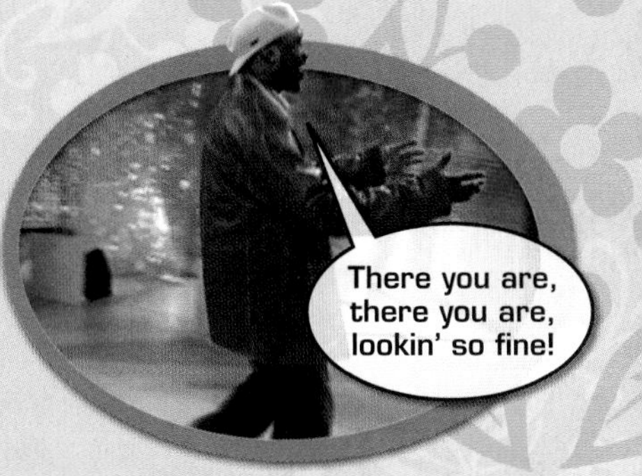
There you are, there you are, lookin' so fine!

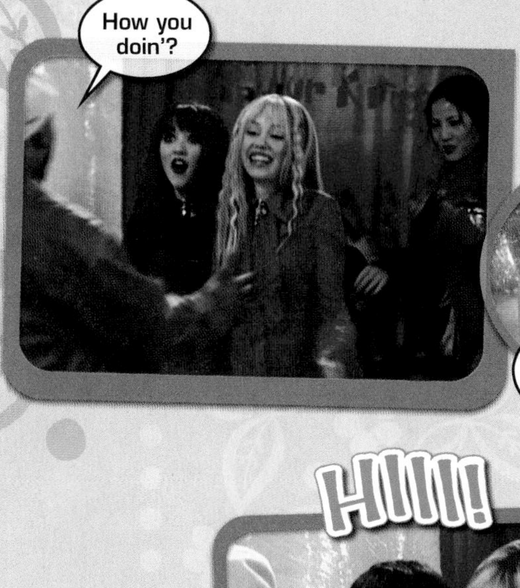
How you doin'?

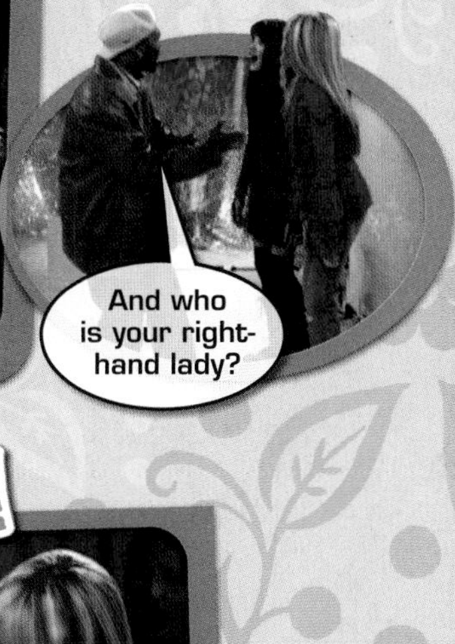
And who is your right-hand lady?

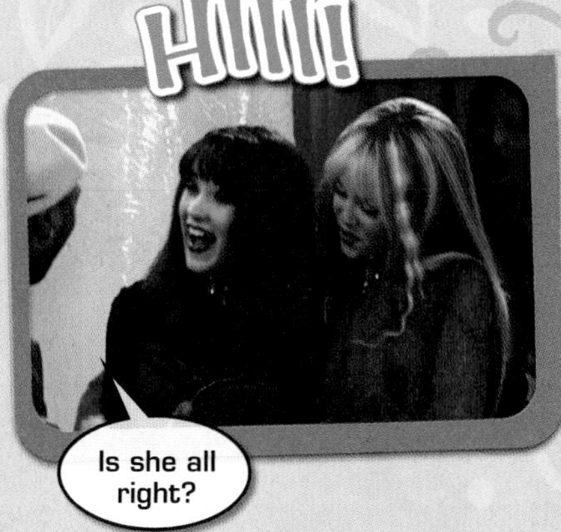
HIIII!
Is she all right?

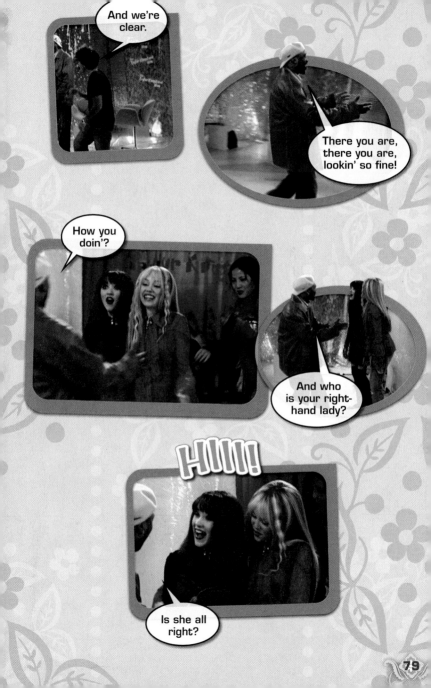

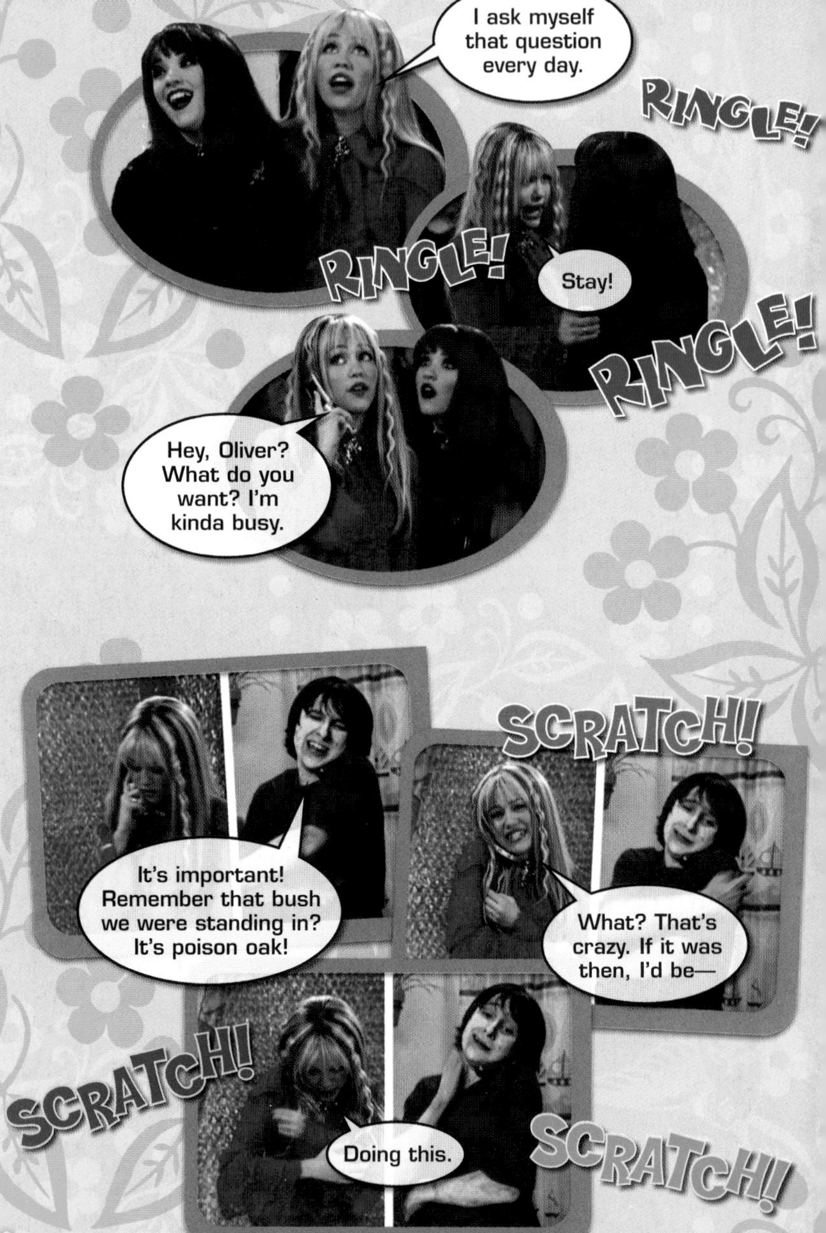
I ask myself that question every day.
RINGLE!
RINGLE!
Stay!
RINGLE!
Hey, Oliver? What do you want? I'm kinda busy.
It's important! Remember that bush we were standing in? It's poison oak!
SCRATCH!
What? That's crazy. If it was then, I'd be—
SCRATCH!
Doing this.
SCRATCH!

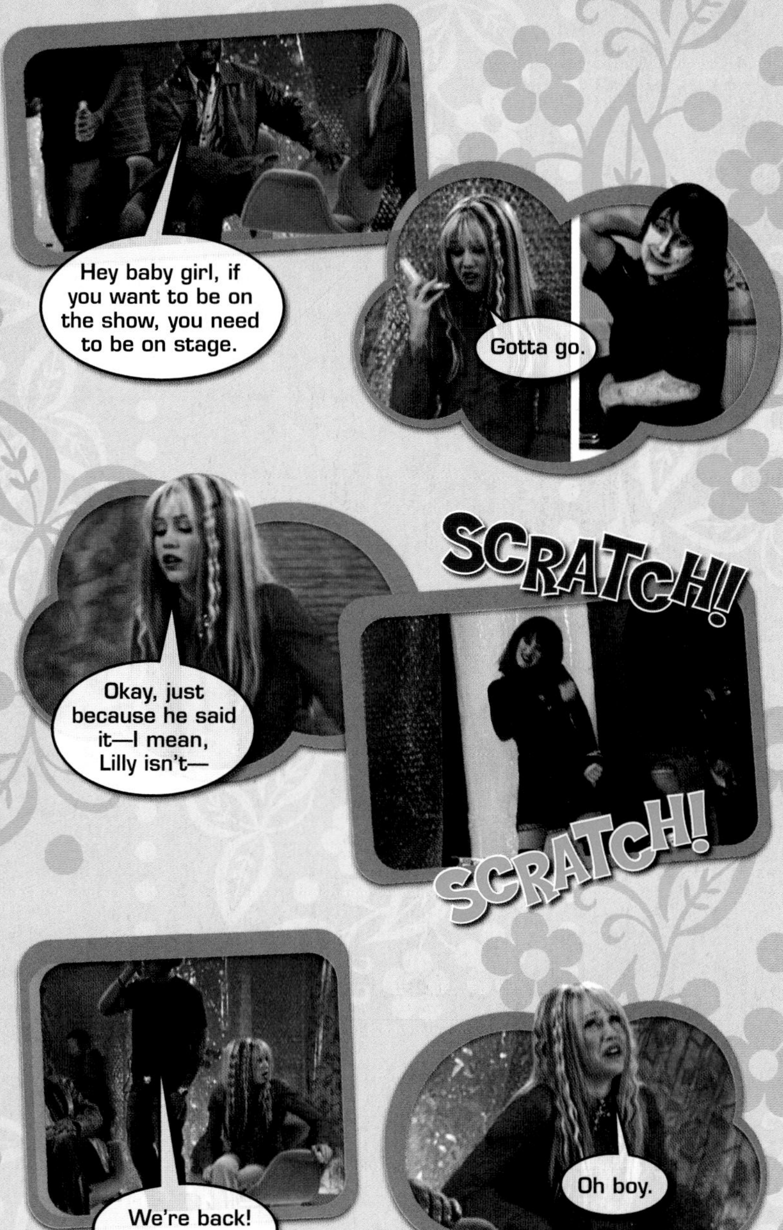
Hey baby girl, if you want to be on the show, you need to be on stage.
Gotta go.
Okay, just because he said it—I mean, Lilly isn't—
SCRATCH!
SCRATCH!
We're back! Three, two...
Oh boy.

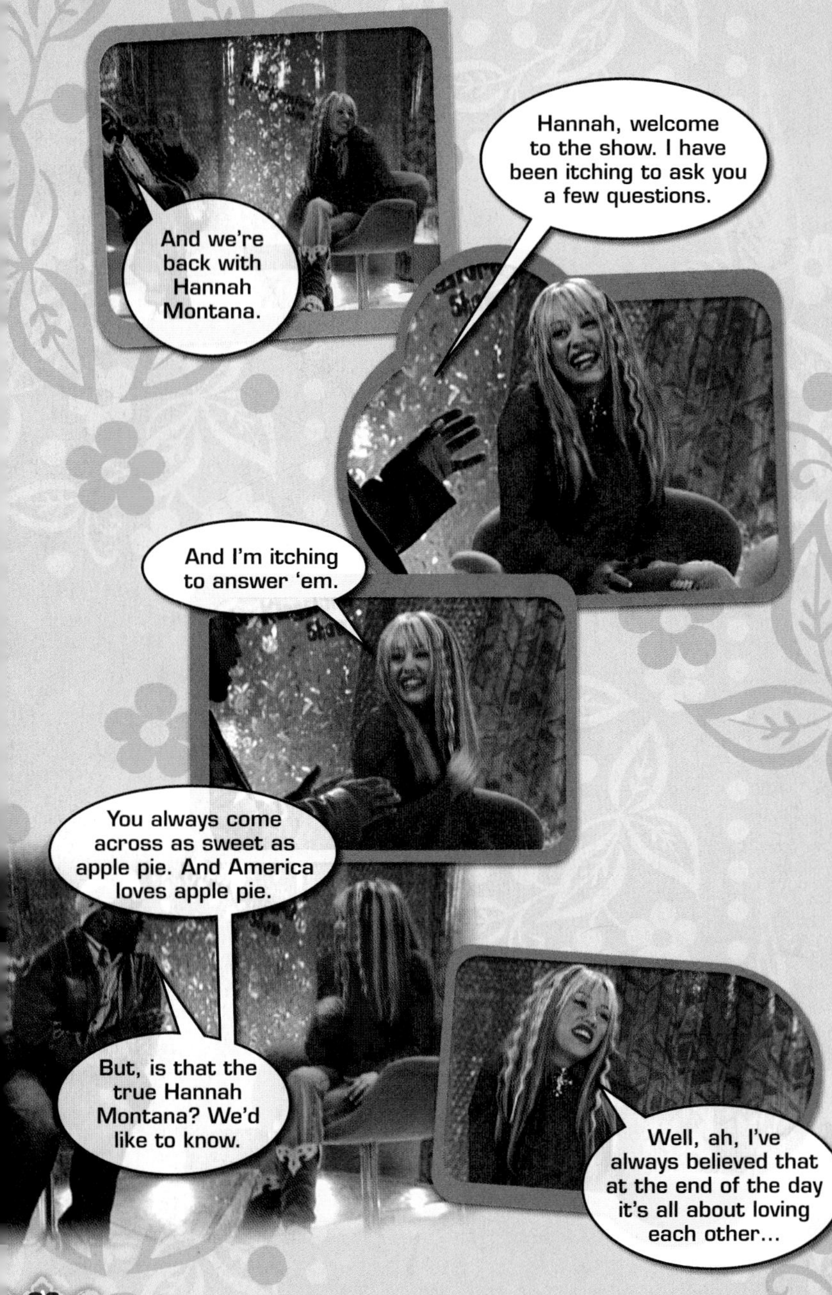
And we're back with Hannah Montana.
Hannah, welcome to the show. I have been itching to ask you a few questions.
And I'm itching to answer 'em.
You always come across as sweet as apple pie. And America loves apple pie.
But, is that the true Hannah Montana? We'd like to know.
Well, ah, I've always believed that at the end of the day it's all about loving each other...

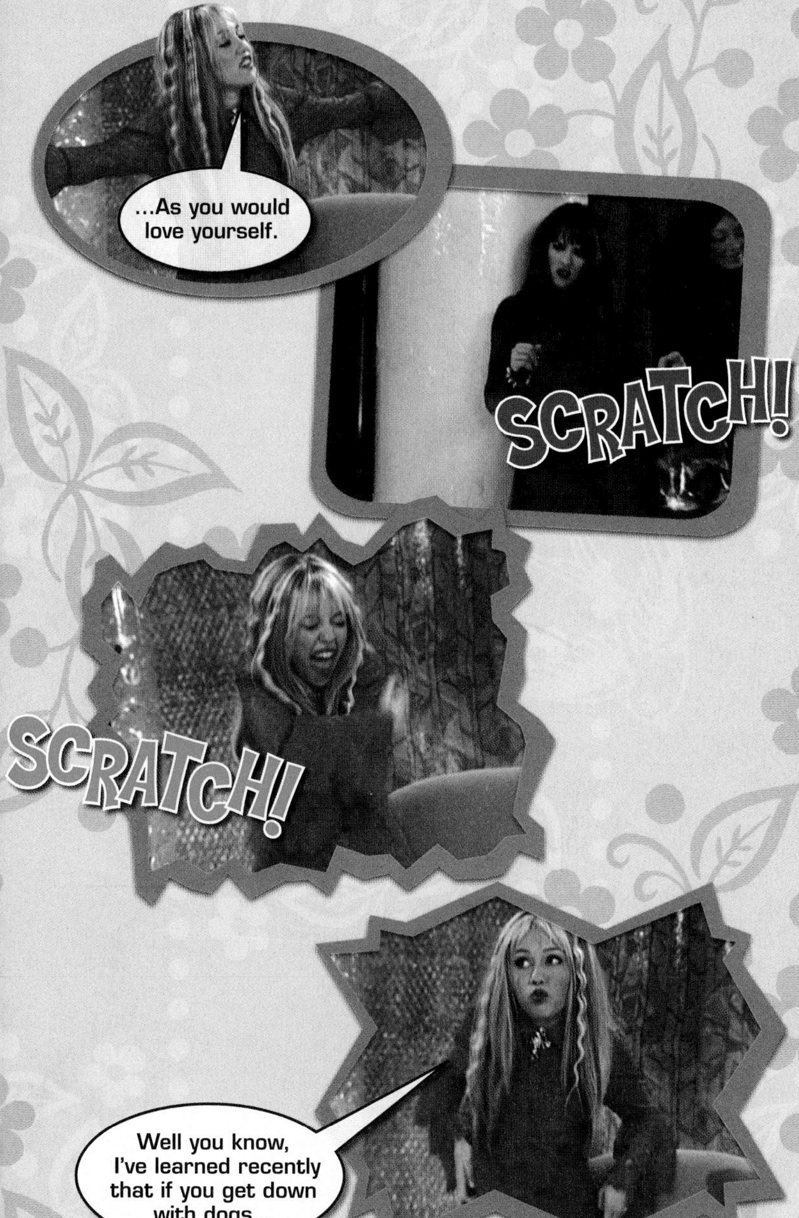
...As you would love yourself.
SCRATCH!
SCRATCH!
Well you know, I've learned recently that if you get down with dogs...

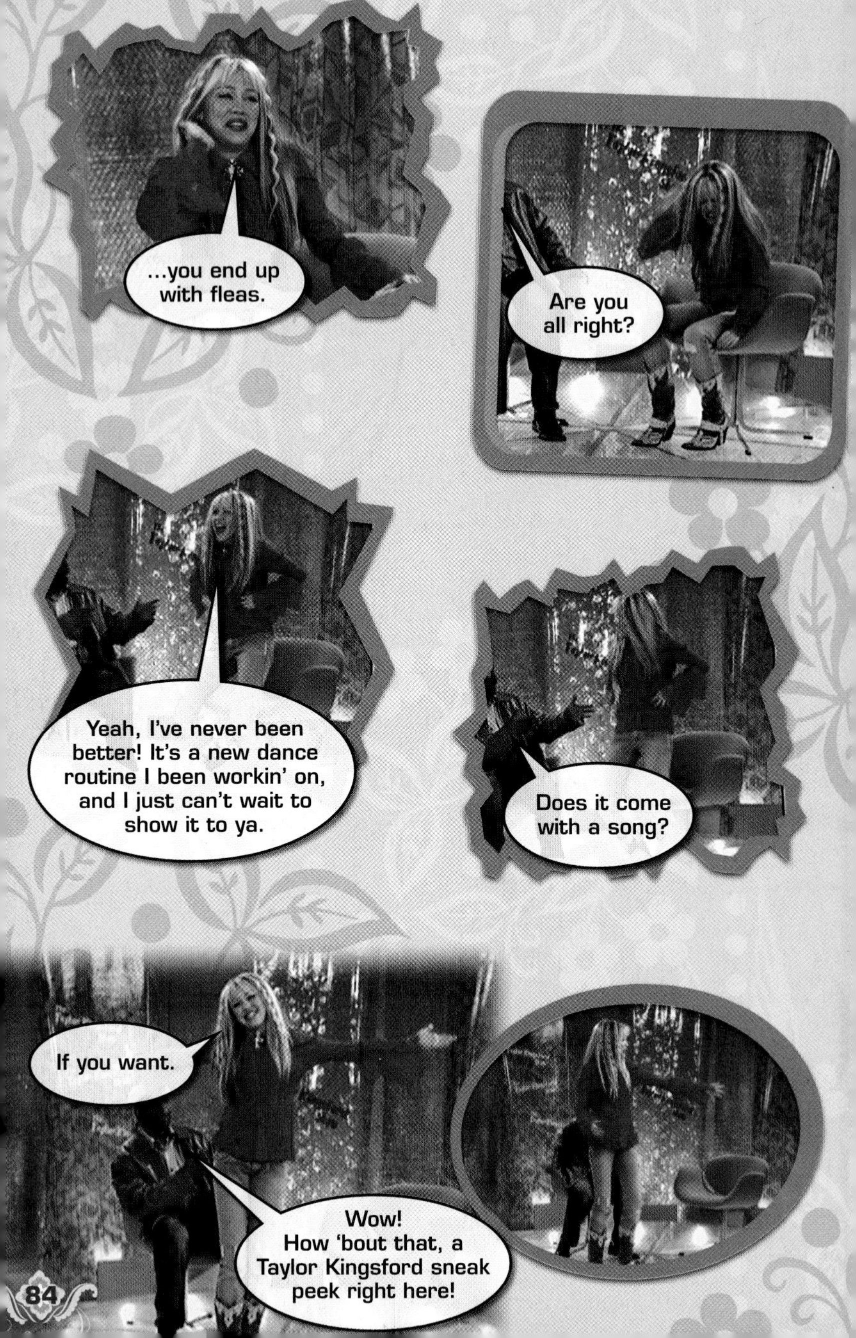

...you end up with fleas.
Are you all right?
Yeah, I've never been better! It's a new dance routine I been workin' on, and I just can't wait to show it to ya.
Does it come with a song?
If you want.
Wow! How 'bout that, a Taylor Kingsford sneak peek right here!

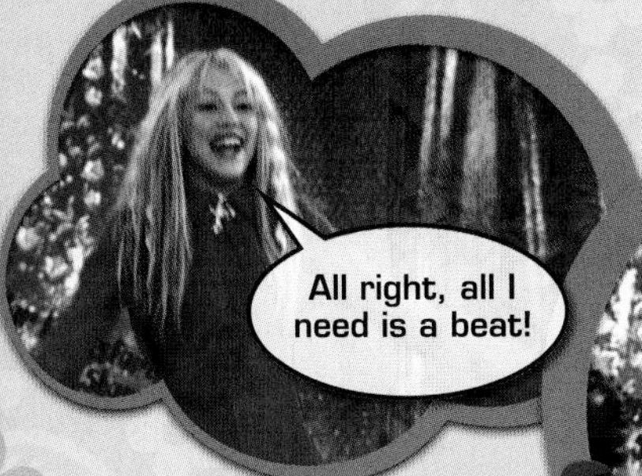
All right, all I need is a beat!
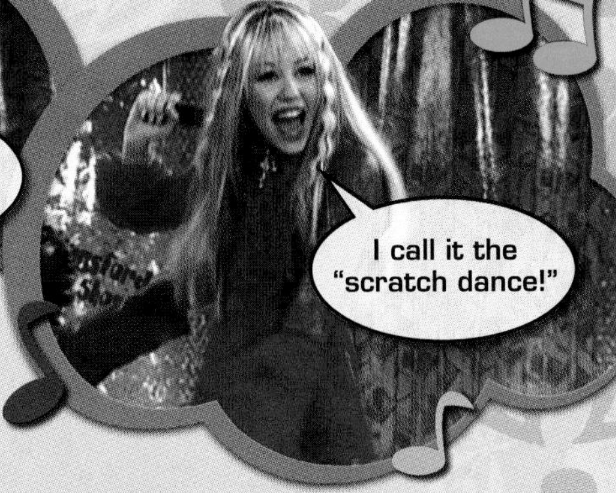
I call it the "scratch dance!"
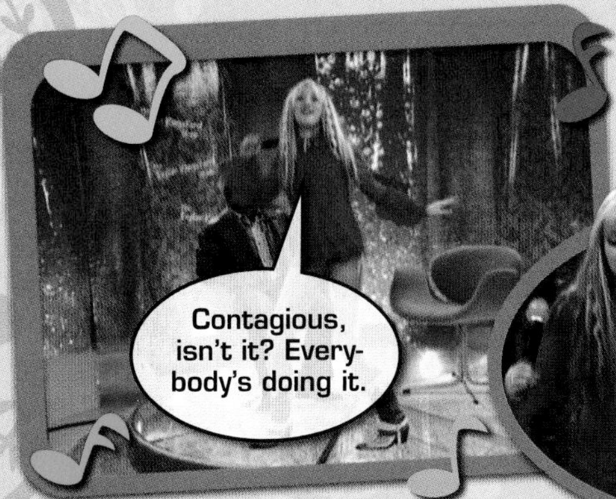
Contagious, isn't it? Every-body's doing it.
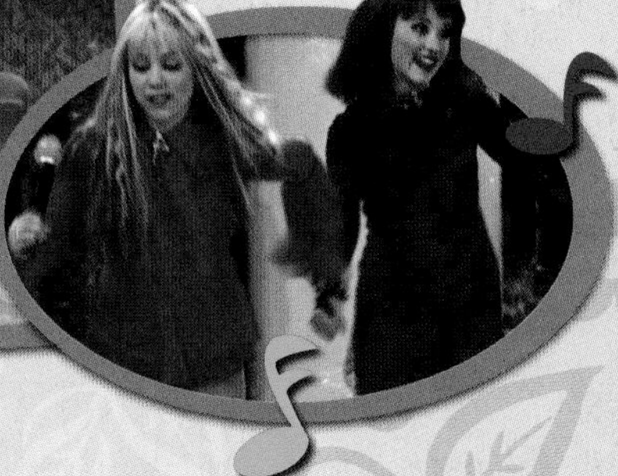
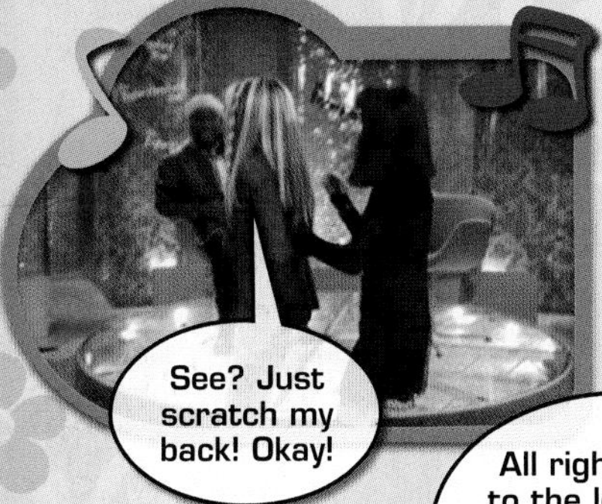
See? Just scratch my back! Okay!
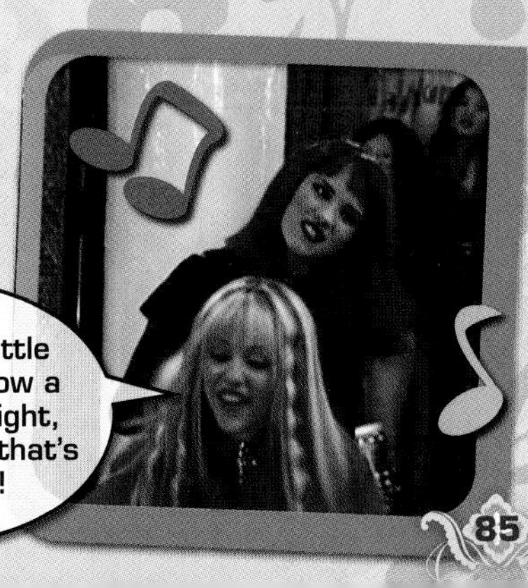
All right! A little to the left, now a little to the right, higher, lower, that's just right!

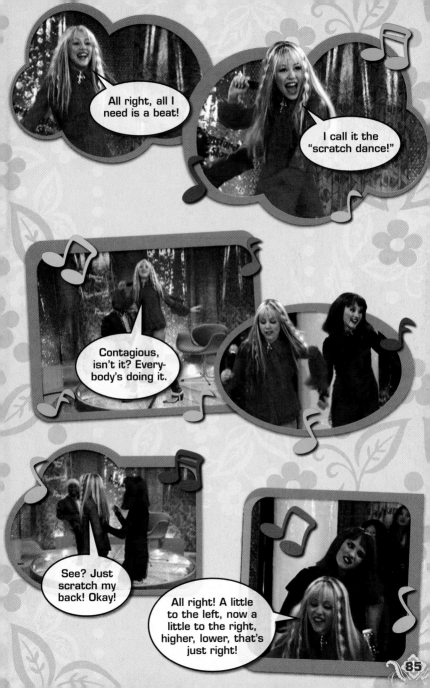

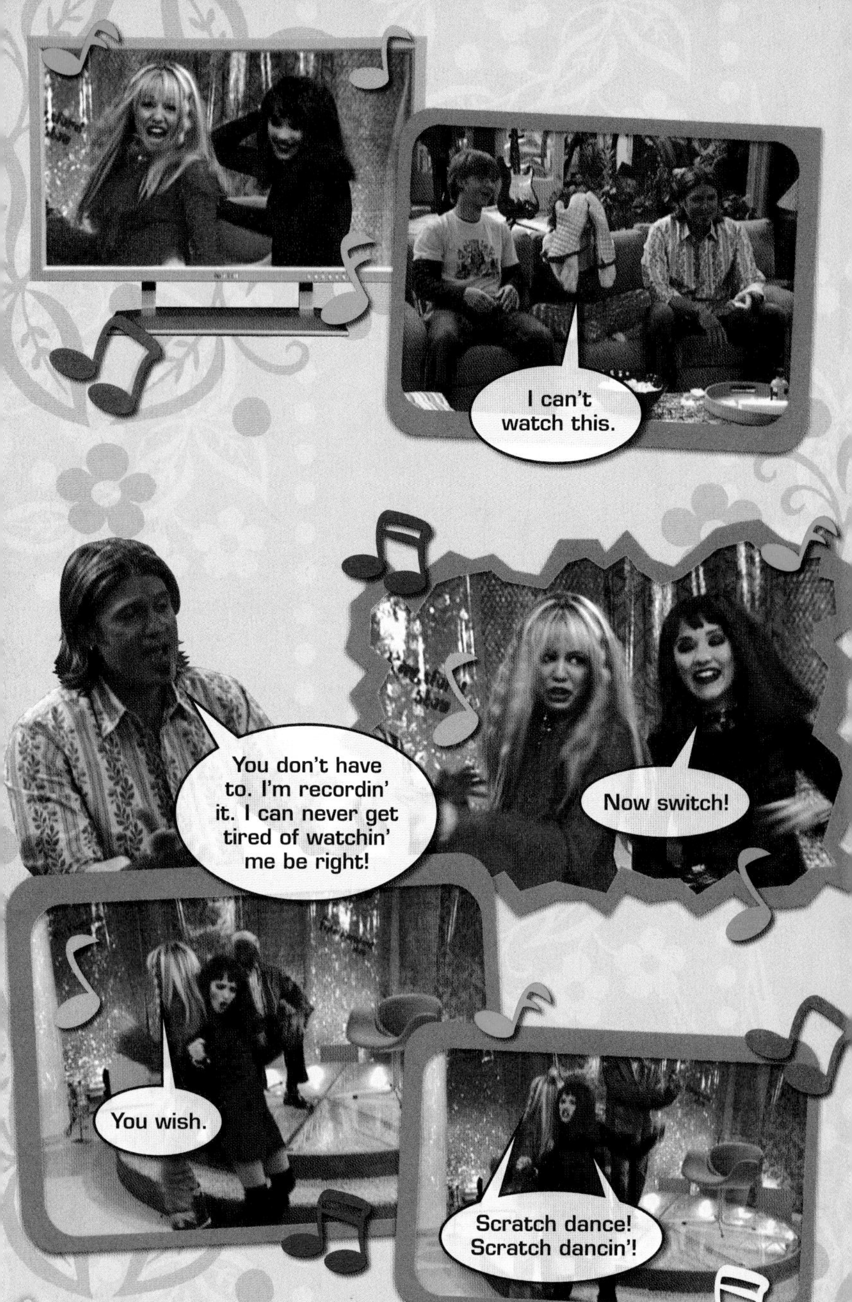
I can't watch this.
You don't have to. I'm recordin' it. I can never get tired of watchin' me be right!
Now switch!
You wish.
Scratch dance! Scratch dancin'!

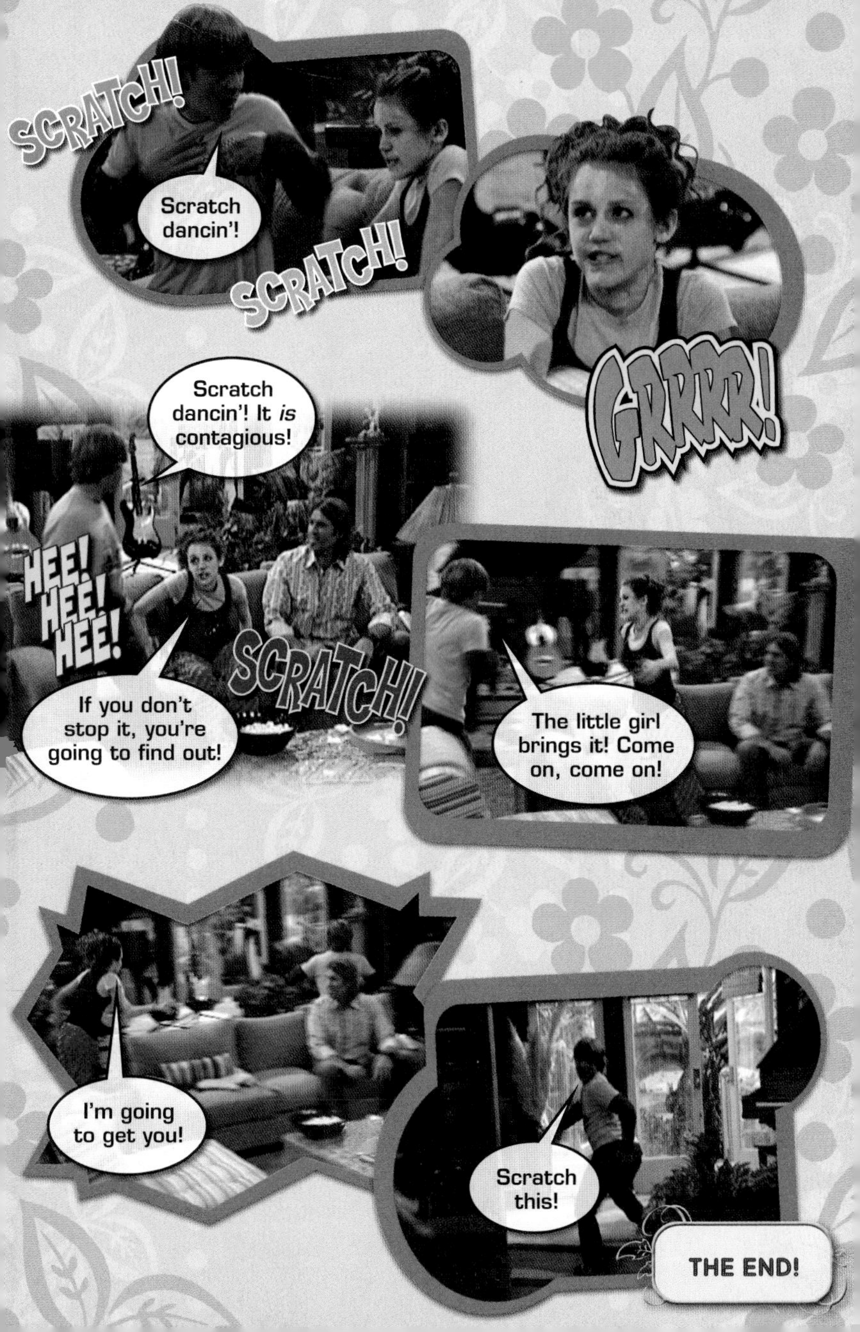
SCRATCH!
Scratch dancin'!
SCRATCH!
GRRRR!
Scratch dancin'! It *is* contagious!
HEE! HEE! HEE!
If you don't stop it, you're going to find out!
SCRATCH!
The little girl brings it! Come on, come on!
I'm going to get you!
Scratch this!
THE END!

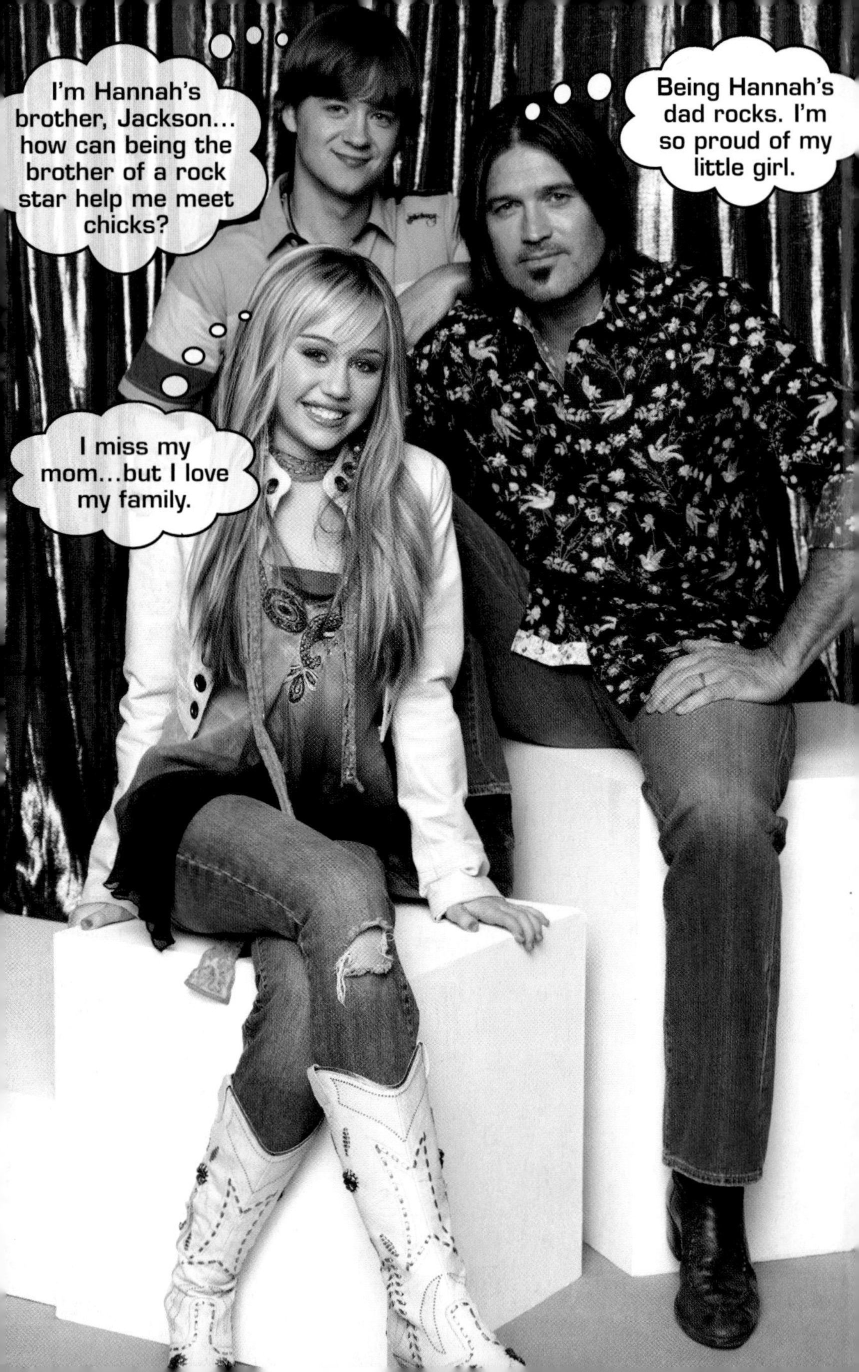
I'm Hannah's brother, Jackson... how can being the brother of a rock star help me meet chicks?
Being Hannah's dad rocks. I'm so proud of my little girl.
I miss my mom...but I love my family.

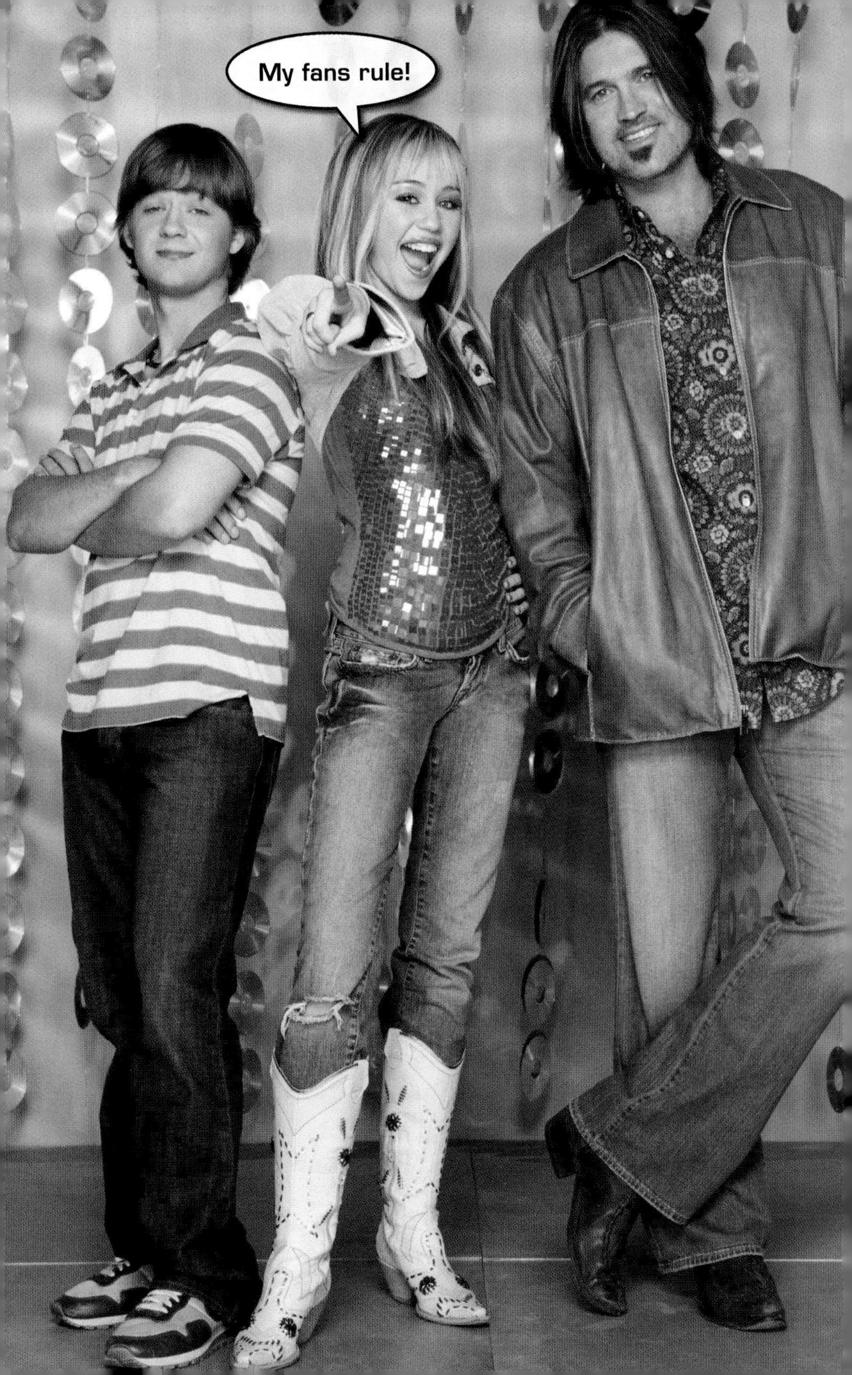
My fans rule!